AS THE
BOMBS
FELL

My Childhood During the
Time the Nazis Ruled

Otto Schmalz

FriesenPress

Suite 300 - 990 Fort St
Victoria, BC, V8V 3K2
Canada

www.friesenpress.com

ISBN
978-1-5255-3626-7 (Hardcover)
978-1-5255-3627-4 (Paperback)
978-1-5255-3628-1 (eBook)

1. History, Social History

Distributed to the trade by The Ingram Book Company

Table of Contents

FOREWORD

Some of the stories you'll find in this book were my bed-time stories as a child. I was born in Canada in a safe, happy environment. So hearing what my parents went through when they were my age was fascinating! The tales were almost incomprehensible as they were such a stark contrast with my own experience. I always pleaded, "tell me a story of the olden days!"

I couldn't help but be impressed by how brave my father had to be as a child; given the circumstances he was thrust into. I think it played a role in how resilient and determined he has always been. His drive and sense of commitment throughout his life has been an inspiration for me.

Although strong willed, he is a caring, generous man, who has become more and more affected by today's environmental and economic crises and conflicts around the world. I can't help but think that his own experiences of having so little during the war, and the suffering he bore witness to, shaped his empathetic and now passionate views about our world today.

As an adult, when thinking of having a family of my own, I wanted a record of my father's life experience to be captured so that it can be passed to future generations. Dad indulged my request to write things down. I hope you enjoy the book and find the insight and inspiration that I do.

Linda Schmalz

CHAPTER ONE
About my Parents, and my Own Beginnings

As for my beginnings, the story goes, as told by my mother, that for days the rain fell heavily, and my parents found themselves with nothing to do but fool around. It must have been June 1931. My parents had rented a tent on Waterlooplatz square in Hannover where the annual Schützenfest was celebrated, a huge fair like the Canadian National Exhibition in Toronto. My father sold poultry and game – his business was called "Wild-und Geflügel-Handlung – en gros & en detail" – and he was hoping to make a handsome profit selling *gebratene Hänchen*, roasted cockerels. The fair had originated hundreds of years before, when bow-and-arrow championships were the main attraction. Now there were just a handful of shooting booths but plenty of other amusements, such as rides and eateries.

That year, the fair turned out to be a financial disaster. It rained buckets, flooding the fairgrounds in a half-foot of water. My parents could not afford to go home; they lived in a rented house in a farm village 30 km away. At that time, transportation was not what it is today. So when the rains came, they were stuck. They had to stay in the water-logged tent, with their seventeen-month-old daughter, for two weeks. My father had to protect his goods, and whatever other belongings they had, from getting stolen. Confined to close quarters day and night, my parents did what young people have done since time began.

Another couple, best friends of my parents, must have done the same around the same time. This couple, who lived in the same farm village as my parents, were well off. They had inherited over a million dollars from relatives in the United States and invested some of their money in Hannover's best-known nightclub, Die Rote Mühle, the city's equivalent of Paris's Moulin Rouge. The male friend, I was told by my mother, liked to drink, as did my father. So, these two were good buddies, which almost spelled disaster for a couple of unborn babies. The millionaire couple already had two boys, and since my father was hell-bent on having a boy himself, he made a pact with his friend that if my mother produced another girl and his friend's wife bore another boy, they would switch the babies. I'm not sure if they actually would have gone through with it, but my mother thought that my father was quite serious about it. As it turned out, the other couple had a girl and my parents had me, Ottchen. This is what my parents called me, to distinguish between my father Otto and me. Ottchen means 'little Otto'.

I believe if my parents had conceived a child even only one week later, that person would not have been exactly like me. So I am ever so grateful to the rain god.

My mother and father had completely different ideas as to what my first name(s) should be. My mother was more imaginative, and whatever names she picked would have been completely out of sync with what my father thought. One day my father came home and proudly announced that he had registered my first names. He then filled my mother in as to what they were: Otto, Friederich, and Wilhelm. Otto, because it was also my father's first name. All three were names of well-known imperial leaders. Otto I, better known as Otto the Great, consolidated the First German Reich and became, as Otto II in 962 AD, the first German emperor of the Holy Roman Empire, which lasted until 1806 – almost a thousand years. The second, Friederich der Grosse (Frederick the Great) was the Prussian king from 1740 to 1786. A brilliant military campaigner and diplomatic strategist, he made Prussia one of the greatest states in Europe. He introduced compulsory schooling for children and brought about many farm reforms. He forced farmers to plant potatoes. Until that time potatoes were not native to Europe; they were introduced from the Americas. Wilhelm II (William II) was the German emperor from 1888 to 1918. Did my father believe that his son would one day become as great as one of those emperors? If so, I'm still waiting for this moment myself.

The rented house in which I was born was called "Sturm's Villa." I don't know whether "Sturm," meaning "storm" in English, was the owner's name or whether it was a nickname for the wooden structure and cladding, which let the wind blow right through it, according to my mother. It was so cold in the living room during the winter that the Christmas tree needles did not fall off. My mother often mentioned that, on March 8th, she took down the Christmas tree just before I came into this world. Women at that time delivered their babies in their homes, especially people who didn't live in big cities. Calling a house a villa suggests that the building is quite a bit above the ordinary and the people living in it are of the better-off classes. This was not the case for the villa where I came into this world. I saw the house from a distance in 1960; it looked more like a wooden house that could have been built in Canada in the nineteenth century.

Otto's Birth-House – Sturm's Villa in Schwüblingsen.
Picture was taken during a visit in 1960.

At this villa my mother would put me outside in a carriage and tie the family dog to it. Bosko was a large black dog. He lay beside the carriage and let no one except my sister, mother or father come near. My sister would play nearby with some neighbour kids and my mother would work in the house and check on us once in a while. In this way, I got exposed to dogs at a very young age and have loved them ever since.

I was also Christened in the little farm village Schüblingsen.

The Church in Schwüblingsen, where Otto was christened in 1932.
Picture taken on 1960 trip to Germany

MY MOTHER

My parents weren't from Hannover. They came from totally different regions and backgrounds. My mother was born in December, 1896 in Gurzno, a small village west of what is now Poznan (Posen in German, which it was at her birth), in Poland. Her father did not have a permanent job. He would go for long periods to the Ruhrgebiet, North Rhine-Westphalia, to work in the coalmines. Her parents, however, also had some land and kept chickens and maybe a couple of pigs. The kids had to help with the work on this miniature farm, and as soon as their years of schooling were done, they had to find work to support the family. My mother's mother died during a miscarriage when my mother was four years old. By that time there were already four brothers and sisters. Her father soon remarried, because he had young kids to look after. The new mother, a young woman, was very nice to all the children she had suddenly inherited, in spite of her husband being very harsh and tough on the whole family. My mother's stepmother also managed to have four more children of her own. So my mother grew up with eight brothers and sisters. I have never seen my mother's parents, or any of her brothers and sisters. My mother did not talk much about them. I only know that one of her sisters moved to France. My mother corresponded with her for a while, but then stopped. My mother said that corresponding with her sister only made her homesick.

* * *

My mother's maiden name was Buchwald. It could be a Jewish name. I may have some Jewish blood running through my veins. If that is so it would not bother me, although I'm sure it would change the way some people would look at me. I have just recently found out how most European Jews got their names, which, after thinking about it a little, tells a lot about the Christian Church, which has had complete control of the way people lived in Europe, at least as far back as the eighteenth century. The Jews at that time were only allowed to live in ghettos in most cities in Europe. It was in the 17th century that it was decided that Jews had to have last names. The Jews were given names that would really stick out and easily identify them as Jews. The names given were Gold, Silver, Stern, Stein, Tannenbaum, Mandelbaum, Katz, Hirsch, Weiss, Weisskopf, Grün and Grünspan, etc. (gold, silver, star, stone, spruce tree, almond tree, cat, deer, white, white head, green and verdigris etc.). Later on, until the Nazis took over in 1933, Jews were allowed to make minor changes in their names, which cost large amounts of money. How much different was this type of name assignment by the Christian authorities in the 17th century from the compulsory wearing of the Judenstern (the yellow star) enforced by the Nazis after the Second World War broke out? My father had several Jewish customers before the Second World War, but my parents never told my sister or me anything about Jews. Parents in Germany were actually afraid of saying the wrong things to their kids, who might by accident repeat them to the wrong people. During *kristallnacht*, the "Night of Broken Glass" in 1938, my father took me downtown in Hannover to see what was being done, and he said to me that it was wrong what the Nazis were doing. I only remember one occasion where I met Jews on the street at the beginning of the war. There were a couple of Jewish teenage boys with stars on their jackets coming towards my friends and I; we were all walking on the sidewalk. When they were about twenty feet in front of us, the boys stepped off the sidewalk and into the street. They walked in the street until they were about ten feet behind us before they stepped back onto the sidewalk.

* * *

My mother told me one story that has stayed in my mind. One Saturday night in her small town there was a dance. A girl who perhaps had overexerted herself gobbled down some cottage cheese and collapsed. Everyone thought that she had died. They placed her in a coffin and put it in a room in the church that was often used for storing dead bodies until they were ready for burial. However, a young man who had been at the dance noticed that the girl's golden necklaces had not been removed, and in the early morning he went to the church to steal them. As he lifted the girl's head, out popped a lump of cheese from her mouth. The man, thinking he had seen a ghost, panicked and ran away. The girl, to the pleasant surprise of everyone, arrived home before daybreak that Sunday morning. The thief was later identified by the girl. My mother did not know whether he received any punishment. If he had not lifted the girl's head the way he did, she might have suffocated. Or worse, she could have wound up getting buried alive.

The area where my mother was born in 1896, was about 100 km west of Poznan, and was part of Germany. At that time, the eastern border was between Germany and Russia, and was some 350 km away from Berlin. Although most schools there taught in German, there were some Polish schools as well, and my mother also learned Polish. So, my mother stayed bilingual – German/Polish – all her life. However, when Germany lost the First World War, a large portion of eastern Germany and a strip of Russia was taken away to create a new Poland. Basically, Poland didn't exist from 1772 until 1918 when, mainly due to France's support, a new state was created. Germany's eastern border was now only 175 km east of Berlin. These new boundaries laid the groundwork for the next territorial dispute, namely Germany's demands for access to its cut-off East Prussian Province. German States or Provinces were actually called Gaue (the name was used in medieval times; it was similar to an English shire) during the Nazi era. The placement of Poland's western border moved again after the Second World War, when the whole of Poland was moved even further west, to within 70 km of Berlin. The Soviet Union's border came also west to give the Soviets access to the Baltic Sea.

Over the centuries, powers, no matter who they were, always had to move some of their citizens into the newly conquered territories to make it easier to hold on to them. That is how the whole world has been migrating back and forth. Two hundred years back, eastern European countries saw great influxes of Germans because their governments invited them. Easterners from as far as Asia have moved west, and the Europeans colonized North and South America. There is no other species that has moved in order to gain more territory. All other species on earth, when they move into a new territory, give up the areas where they had just been. What does this tell us about the human race?

* * *

So my mother, before the First World War, was living in what had then been part of Germany for more than one hundred years. In 1913, just before the First World War started, she decided to go to the state of Westphalia in the Rhine valley to find work. At that time, children went to school until they were fourteen, and then found jobs to support their family. So my mother, and any sisters and brothers who still lived at home, had to hand over whatever they earned to their parents. The only way they could keep their earnings was to move out. The best place to go for better-paying jobs at that time was the Rhineland in southwest Germany. My mother found a job working as a domestic in an industrialist's household in Vohwinkel, in Westphalia. Now a suburb of the city of Wuppertal I believe. So, during WW I she, as a teenager and then a young woman, grew up and lived more than 650 km away from her family. She had nothing but pleasant memories about that workplace. It was a home away from home. The industrialist was very wealthy – I believe he owned a steel mill – and he and his family treated their staff very well. On many occasions my mother spoke of how well the sons treated the servants.

One of her experiences at that place that sticks in my mind is this: my mother hurt her lower leg and it was actually healed by a gypsy woman. The wound had been looked at by some medical experts and had received some sort of treatment, but it would not get better. It actually got worse over time and eventually became quite a hole that oozed puss galore. No one knew what to do about it. Then one day, as happened every once in a while, a gypsy woman came to the door to beg for food and whatever else she could get. My mother let her into the house while she looked for something to give her. The gypsy woman, seeing the bandage on my mother's leg, asked what was wrong with it. My mother showed her the wound. The woman suggested that my mother try an unconventional treatment – she should take her own faeces and put it into the wound. She was to bandage the wound and repeat the treatment every day until the wound was healed. My mother could not bring herself to tell anyone about this. But she was desperate enough to try it. So she put her own faeces into the wound, and voilà, in a few days the wound started to heal.

During the first years after WW I, it was impossible for my mother to travel to see her parents in the newly recreated Poland. Whatever money my mother might have saved became almost worthless because of the post-war conditions dictated to Germany. The German mark was not accepted as currency outside of Germany.

According to the stories my mother told me, in the early 1920s she fell madly in love with a handsome young man. She never mentioned his name. When she talked about him she always said "my fiancée." This fellow was a house painter, but not of the ordinary type. He was more of an artist than a plain painter. Wallpaper was not used like it is today. So people who could afford it would have artists paint large landscapes or religious scenes on their living room, or especially bedroom, walls. He was that sort of a painter. My mother was engaged to him. However, she had known him for less than two years when he died of pneumonia. My mother knew a German song about a house painter; it must have been on the hit parade at the time. She sang or hummed it even in her eighties. The song went something like:

Mein Man ist Maler
verdient am Tag drei Thaler
Maler, Maler, Maler, Maler
Maler ist mein Man.

This translates into:

My man is a painter
He earns per day three Thaler
painter, painter, painter, painter
painter is my man.

A Thaler was a former German silver coin, worth about three German Marks.

My mother must have been crazily in love with that man. I believe he was her first love. The only other thing I know about her fiancée is that his father was a heavy drinker who treated his wife very badly. He would beat her often. The father was a coal miner. One day he told his wife that he would outlive her, and that she would not live much longer. That day he went to work and never came home. He was in a cage going down the mineshaft when the operator controlling the hoist from above dropped the cage too far by mistake. It dipped into the water at the bottom of the pit. Everyone stayed in the cage except the fiancée's father. Just as he started to climb out the operator noticed that the cage had gone too far and switched it to the up direction, cutting the man in half.

A good-looking, but somewhat shy woman, my mother did not want to be a domestic forever. In 1929, she answered a newspaper ad for work cutting asparagus. The asparagus in Germany and throughout Europe is a different type than in North America. This asparagus is white, and its texture is a little softer. It almost melts in one's mouth. It is seeded a foot deep in a ridge of soft sandy soil. The land where asparagus is planted looks bare; one sees only foot-high ridges of soil. The farmer has to keep an eye on the field in order to detect when the asparagus is ready to break through the top. As soon as the asparagus sticks its head out of the ground, it is too late; the asparagus then turns green, woody and not fit to eat. Normally, the asparagus is ripe for cutting in May. Often a large area has to be harvested at once, and it can be hard to get enough people together in a hurry. The asparagus is cut by plunging an eighteen-inch-long knife into the ground and hopefully cutting it off at the bottom.

My mother, who knew this asparagus harvest procedure, travelled about 300 km by train to answer the ad. She discovered that the gentleman who had put the ad in the paper did not own any land. More or less by handshake, he made deals with the farmers to harvest the asparagus and take it to market, mainly in Hannover, a city with a population of close to a half a million. When my mother went for the interview, this gentleman told her that she was too good for this kind of work. Her hands were too delicate, he said. He promised to find some other work for her.

He was a smooth talker, and my mother was shy and inexperienced. She hadn't had a relationship with a man since her fiancée died a few years earlier. So, abra cadabra, my mother was made pregnant by this gentleman, only to find out that he was still married to another woman. However, before my sister was born in January 1930, the man, my father, got his divorce.

My mother was born a Catholic, whereas my father was a Lutheran Protestant. When they got married, my father was not going to change his religion, so they had to marry as Protestants, and consequently my mother was excommun-icated from the Catholic Church.

When my sister, Hannelore, was about six months old, she contracted whooping cough. It lasts about ten weeks and can be fatal. This prompted my mother to go and show her daughter to her parents. As already mentioned, the region where her parents lived had become part of Poland after the First World War. So my mother, with her sick six-month-old baby, had to cross the border to enter Poland. She told me once that the treatment on the train, going through customs, was much better from the Polish officers than the Germans. They were so helpful with her baby and all.

By this time, in 1930, my parents lived in the small town called Lehrte, about 25 km from Hannover. My father just could not stay in one spot for long. As my mother often suggested, my father lacked Sitzfleisch (the ability to sit still); instead, he seemed to have Pfeffer im Arsch (pepper up his rear end). Before I was born, my parents had already moved to the small farm village, Schwüblingsen where I came into this world in March 1932.

My Father

My father, also not a 'Hannoveraner', was born in March 1898 in the small city of Halberstadt, north of the Harz Mountains, in the northern central part of Germany. I don't know anything about the city of his childhood, except that today a specially built organ called "ORGAN^2/ASLSP (meaning "as slow as possible") 1985" is playing a work for solo piano composed by John Cage on the organ of St. Burchardi Church. The piece started on September 5, 2001, on what would have been Cage's 98th birthday, and it will play in this church for 639 years to commemorate the lifespan of the first modern Blockwerk organ, which was built in the Halberstadt Church in 1361 and lasted until the millennium. Because it is playing so slow, it may take 2 months before the organ switches from playing one note to playing the next note. One can perhaps hear the same note 24 hours a day for months. This is an international effort, thought up by a group of musicologists and philosophers from around the world. It could easily be considered as a silly project, but compared to other international projects involving exploitation, domination and war; we would have heaven on earth if we turned our energy only to silly projects like this.

Like other kids at the time, my father left school at the age of fourteen. He then learned cooking and baking, and became a cook and pastry chef. This was probably one of the best professions he could have taken up. He was a small man, shorter than my mother, perhaps not much more than five feet tall. He was always full of mischief, and often bragged about it. When he was a little boy, he one time took small ducklings and stuck their heads into the mud. When he let them go, they would wobble like drunks. He thought it was funny.

When the First World War broke out, my father was conscripted into the German army as a cook. One has to imagine what field cooking for the army was like in the First World War. Field kitchens still had mobile cauldrons with fire boxes underneath. My father liked to be in charge and organize, instead of having to work himself. My mother always said that he had two left hands and that he was clumsy with tools. My mother was the worker in the house. Consequently, he must have been more involved in the food rationing and the food and fuel supply problems than today's army cooks.

He spent most of the war at the western front. He claimed, and I believe him that he was slightly wounded, and at one point he was buried alive. He always blamed his asthma and hair loss on being buried alive, and on gas poisoning.

That brings me to the use of gas in the First World War. Today, and for some time, the British, Canadian and American news media always report that Germany was the first to use poison gas in the Great War. However, at the time, the presses in the West, from London to as far away as Australia, wrote that the first gas attacks were conducted by the French in the early days of the war, (as described in *Two Thousand Questions And Answers About The War*, published by George H. Doran Company, USA 1918). The war started on June 28, 1914. According to the book, London newspaper reports dated September 14, 1914, quoted the French inventor, M. Turpin, describing how terrifying and deadly his gas (turpinite) was, and how its use had been approved by the French War Minister. According to the dispatches, whole companies of German soldiers died so quickly on the explosion of these gas shells that the dead were found in exactly the attitude of life. Papers in the US and Australia praised the marvellous effects the gas had on German soldiers. However it was later proven that the use of this supposedly deadly gas turpinite was a myth.

In the on-line publication *History of Chemical/ Biological Arms Race*: Chapter-One" Lenny Flank wrote on 2013/09/06: "- - - - By the 19th century, military leaders began to investigate the possibility of routinely using poisonous chemicals as standardized weapons. Instead of the makeshift CBW attacks which had been carried out previously, new and more modern methods of utilizing poisons were sought. - - - By the time of the Boer War in Africa in 1889, most of the world's military establishments were conducting serious research into the widespread use of chemical and biological weapons. - - - The British, however, did use the Boer War to test a new chemical device of their own. This was an artillery shell filled with picric acid, which, after impact, released the explosive gas lyddite. The British encountered a host of technical problems with the new weapons, however, and they proved to be practically worthless."

In "100 Years of Tear Gas – The Atlantic" Anna Feigenbaum wrote on Aug 16, 2014: "*In August 1914, French troops fired tear-gas grenades into German trenches along the border between the two countries. While the exact details of this first tear-gas launch are fuzzy, historians mark the Battle of the Frontiers, as World War I's first clashes between France and Germany came to be known, as the birthday of what would become modern tear gas.*"

Could one speculate that the prevailing atmosphere over the decades leading up to this point, as well as these a foregoing events prompted Germany to get into this type of warfare in a bigger way? After all, their first release of chlorine gas happened a full nine months after the breakout of the First World War, on April 22, 1915.

The question that people should ask themselves is; why do we have to kill each other? When dissecting the reasons used for humans killing humans they all seem to boil down to one thing and that is greed. The man killing his wife or wife's lover is because of possession, he does not want to share her. In some places women are still traded for goods, and kept like slaves. These women don't have rights and may lose their lives if they are caught with another man even if it is a rape. Humans are killing other humans to get ahold of their possessions. People are killing people to ensure that stuff is not taken from them. When governments tell their people to make war against other people it is that they want to have what the other people possess. In some cases, believing that the other side is preparing for war, governments seek first-strike advantage, so they have the upper hand. If they win, they will not lose some of their own possessions. If a country tries to harm or attack another country because it is becoming too strong economically for them, that boils down to greed as well. People followed their kings' orders for millennia. Europeans have killed and taken stuff (land, slaves, gold, and other resources) from natives all over America, Australia, New Zeeland, India and Africa over the last few centuries. Within Europe and Asia, people have been doing this to each other for millennia.

The idea of "winner takes all" is accepted by a lot people in sports, politics and life in general. It is so wrong, and damaging to the majority of the remaining people. We could have paradise on earth if humans could only share their wealth.

However, with respect to how we incapacitate or kill our enemy, one really has to question how inadequately the human mind works when it tries to reason things out. It looks like we have to categorize killings into necessary killings at certain times and for certain things. For instance, something might be considered a crime in some places, but the same person may be highly rewarded for the same deed in other places. There were times when executions were done publicly and people would come to witness with pleasure a person being torn apart by a lion, hanged or beheaded etc. Now we seemed to want to kill certain people in some places humanely with as few witnesses as possible, as long as we kill them.

Why do humans have the need to watch killings in movies and on TV series? If there was no such demand that portion of the huge industry producing them would not exist. Hockey team owners have "enforcers" on their teams to beat up opposing players. The reason given for having these enforcers is that the audience likes to see it, its part of the game.

How can humans think and say the killing of perhaps millions in the dropping of one atomic bomb on a large city is all right as long as we can claim it was done in our defence or for retaliation? Countries keep those weapons in stock. The one country that is the most against other countries having such weapons is also the only one that has ever used such a weapon. Weapons over time have become more and more sophisticated. That does not mean that they kill more humanely (how can any killing be humane?) It may mean the new weapons are more efficient, but in what, killing a greater number and/or at a greater distance?

The use of chemical biological weapons (CBW) has been mentioned in warfare going back thousands of years. It looks like the objection humans have in using CBW stems from the fact that they cannot see the threat coming, which consequently makes it is harder to come up with a proper defence against it in sufficient time. If it weren't for this I'm sure it would be even more readily accepted as a means to kill. Some people who are for the death penalty actually accept using chemicals as a means to kill a person who is found guilty and sentenced to death. Something must have happened to Homo sapiens that caused their brains to function differently from other species. They seem to have this one tiny corner in their brain involved in greedy thinking. Maybe someday in the future it will be found and sapped.

Other creatures have used chemical and biological stunning or killing in order to capture and eat or defend themselves. For these creatures it's always been for food or defence, never for possession.

* * *

It just struck me and I can't hold it back – I agree with the Jews that the Nazi-created holocaust has to be talked about and never be forgotten. In that sense, the stories of all wrongdoings have to be told and repeated again and again. The problem is, no one is willing to admit and talk about one's own wrongdoings. This to me was perhaps instilled in people's minds mainly by the teachings of the Bible more than two millennia ago. The Israelites were told again and again by god, through his (so-called) representatives, to go and kill the people that lived in Canaan (Israel) and establish their kingdom of Israel and eventually rule the whole world. The way it looks, the Jews did not follow the Old Testament's advice, but the Christians did for at least 1500 years. During the crusades Jews were killed by Christians in Europe as well as in the Middle East. According to the well-known British historian Simon Schama, in his "History of Britain" books and TV series, the first time the word "holocaustum" was used outside of the Bible, was when Jews in England were massacred around 1189 to free England of the

Jews. The same was repeated again in England about 100 years later. Germany has a Holocaust Remembrance Day and hundreds of monuments throughout Germany reminding Germans about the wrongs they did. Only South Africa is also reminding its citizens about the wrongs of Apartheid. Canada put up a monument about the Communist victims in Russia, but should Canada not have put up a monument to its own aboriginal victims first?

* * *

After the First World War, when my father started his Wild-und Geflügel-Handlung (poultry and game) business in 1921, the economic conditions in Germany, in which he tried to make a living for himself, were very bad. That originally caused him also to sell all kinds of vegetables, whatever vegetables were in harvest.

Not only my father, but nearly all Germans were having a hard time in the 1920s. By the end of the First World War Germany was heavily in debt. As a result, by 1919 Germany was no longer the second most economically advanced nation in the world. The immediate economic consequences of the especially oppressive terms of the 1919 Treaty of Versailles were a significant concern and added to Germany's humiliation. Putting the blame for the war more or less on Germany alone and consequently asking her to pay for the war put such a financial burden on Germany that the whole country went into turmoil.

A German Communist revolt brought about the short-lived Bavarian Soviet Republic being proclaimed on April 6, 1919. After violent suppression by elements of the German Army and, notably, the Freicorps, the Bavarian Soviet Republic fell in May 1919. Consequently, the Bamberger Verfassung (Bamberg Constitution) was enacted in August, 1919, and came into force on September 15, 1919, creating the Free State of Bavaria within the Weimar Republic.

In 1920, Germany was asked to pay 226 milliards (milliard being most Europeans' terminology for billion at that time) in goldmarks (that is, in actual gold bullion) – roughly US$32 billion. The war debt was all to be paid in gold or US dollars, of which Germany had none. This debt load was put on Germany not only to pay off the cost of the war, but to prevent Germany from ever again becoming an industrial and military power. In addition, the country was directed to turn over 26 percent of its exports to pay for the war. This drove German inflation so high that it missed one war payment to France at the end of 1922. As a consequence, in January 1923, French troops occupied Germany's chief industrial region, in the Ruhr valley. This brought about a general strike by German workers.

During the war, in May 1917, 4.2 German paper marks were worth about one US dollar. By November 21, 1923, the value of the mark dropped to an all-time low: 4.21 trillion marks equalled one US dollar. Some sort of stability was only achieved on August 30, 1924 when 1 trillion paper marks were exchanged for one Reichsmark, which became the new German currency. At this point, 4.2 Reichsmarks were equivalent to 1 US dollar.

People say that nothing like that could be repeated today. Well the way things look, the world is not getting better in how countries treat each other. Things seem to be getting worse.

The hopeless conditions in post-war Germany reached a peak in 1923 and gave Adolf Hitler the opportunity to spread his Nazi philosophy. Many happenings led up to this point. In January 1923 the Ruhr Valley occupation by France took place, causing a general strike of German workers. Inflation was so bad that the wages workers received at the end of the day had to be spent as soon as they got them. Because of hyperinflation, that same money was worthless the next day. At first everything was costing in millions, then tens of millions, hundreds of millions and billions. New money was printed daily. Hitler's coup on November 9, 1923 (The Beer Hall Putsch) during which 20 people died came close to succeeding. Hitler's idea was to take over the Free State of Bavaria and use it as a springboard to take over the whole of Germany later. These happenings were all causing tremendous strains on Germany's Weimar Republic. It was Hitler's four-week trial in March 1924, in which he defended himself, that gave him the opportunity to spread his propaganda, by way of all the important German newspapers that covered his trial. It changed politics in Germany. He also used the nine months jail time he served, of the five year sentence he got, to write his *"Mein Kampf"* (My Struggle) book.

In 1925, Germany's conservatives asked the 78-year-old Paul von Hindenburg to be their candidate for second President of the German Republic. He was elected easily. The former Allies feared that he would attempt to restore the Hohenzollerns to the monarchy, but Hindenburg surprised the world by upholding the Weimar Constitution. He agreed to all the policies that would reconcile Germany with its former foes. In the election of 1932, Hindenburg defeated Adolf Hitler, but Hitler got 37 percent of the popular votes and 230 seats of the total 608 seats. He got the biggest single voting bloc. As economic and political conditions in Germany grew worse, with an unemployment rate around 30 percent, Hindenburg finally submitted to Nazi pressure and named Hitler Reich Chancellor of Germany on January 30, 1933. Thereafter Hitler amassed ever-greater power. When Hindenburg died, on August 2, 1934, Hitler took over the presidency, which also made him the commander-in-chief of the armed forces. It was the desperate economic conditions that Germany had to endure for fifteen years, the fear of Communism, plus financial support from England and the United States, that brought Hitler to power.

My father had strong political opinions that never changed during the time I knew him, or at least until I left Germany in 1951. By that time he was already fifty-three. He was a Social Democrat and he would openly talk about it. He never was shy to voice his opinion, and sometimes it got him into a lot of trouble, especially during the time when the Nazis were in power. To backtrack a little, Hitler's party, the NSDAP (National Socialistic German Workers Party) was, by the late twenties, involved almost daily in street fights with the Communists somewhere in Germany. There was a power struggle and these two parties were so aggressive and strong that one of them would come out as the winner and become the governing party of Germany.

The Communists, who had deposed the Russian Tsar and had been ruling Russia for more than ten years by now, were for the establishment in Germany of complete socialism. No private businesses or free presses would be allowed. This was not a system that the industrialists, rich and materialistic- oriented people of Germany and other western countries could allow to take over Germany. As far as these other countries went, they were afraid that this could spread communism throughout Europe. So industrialists in Germany, England and the USA financially supported Hitler's party. From 1930, the up-to-then insignificant NSDAP of Adolf Hitler, which fused extreme anti-democratic tendencies and a raging anti-Semitism with pseudo-revolutionary propaganda, grew from strength to strength, and by 1932 had become Germany's most powerful party, although with only 37 percent of the popular votes.

* * *

In 1934, my father was still trying to make money selling whatever farm produce he could, including asparagus on the open market in Hannover. One of his competitors had a stand selling asparagus right next to my father's. This fellow wanted to get rid of his competition. So he took my father to court, accusing him of false advertising. He said in court that my father claimed that his asparagus came from the town of Burgdorf, when in reality it came from perhaps a dozen villages around Burgdorf. The judge asked my father what he had to say in his defence.

"Your Honour, I gather asparagus from all over the district of Burgdorf," my father said. "I can't see how I can label every little bundle and keep it separate. The asparagus all comes from the District of Burgdorf so I called it Burgdorfer asparagus."

The judge replied, "I agree, case dismissed."

Shortly after that, the same competitive merchant accused my father of wearing a Nazi Party membership button under his lapel. He contended that my father would flash this button when he wanted to impress someone. It is true that my father always wanted to impress people, especially if they were of the female persuasion. However, I don't think he would have gone that far and worn that button, because he was a Social Democrat and hated the Nazis. By this time, Hitler had abolished and outlawed all other parties in Germany, and pretending to be a Nazi Party member, when one was not, had become a crime. So when the case went to court, the accuser had a policeman as witness. The judge told my father that he had to believe the testimony of the honourable policeman, and sentenced my father to six weeks in jail. Unknowingly, President Hindenburg came to my father's rescue. Within days of my father's sentencing, the 87-year-old president died, and Hitler declared an amnesty and pardoned all the more benign of criminals. So my father did not have to go to jail.

CHAPTER TWO
The Years Before School

By that time my parents had moved to the Kramerstrasse, the oldest part of the city of Hannover. Our rented apartment was not far from a castle, perhaps a five-minute walk. The castle called 'Lineschloss' was the residence of Hannover's kings for centuries. It has been rebuilt after it had been totally burned out during the Second World War; it again looks like it did in the 1930s. The kingdom of Hannover goes back hundreds of years. In 1714, when Queen Anne of England died, King George Louis of Hannover became George I, king of England and Hannover. For the next two hundred years, the British kings' and queens' family name was "House of Hannover," and German was taught to all the royal children. However, at the beginning of the First World War, because of strong anti-German feelings in England, the royal name was changed to House of Windsor. I remember, as a little kid, I used to walk through the castle's cavernous passageway and shout. The echoes of my voice always reverberated loud between the walls.

The Kramerstrasse house, in which my parents had rented an upstairs apartment, was likely hundreds of years old.

Kramerstrasse 1934 from left to right
Hannelore-Father-Otto with Teddy Bear

The owner didn't live there and let the place deteriorate. After trying to talk the owner into doing some repair work, without getting results, my father took the owner to court. My father thought it was fun going to court, and when he was asked by the judge to describe the conditions, he tried to make a joke. He told the judge that, when he came home around one or two o'clock in the morning after visiting his customers, rats would scurry down the stairs and greet him with "Heil Hitler." The judge's immediate response was that he did not hear him properly, but that he did not want him to repeat whatever he had said. My father never told me whether he won or lost the case. My guess is that the case was thrown out after the kind of statement my father made. If he had done the same thing five years later, he probably would have wound up in prison.

Not long after this court case, my parents moved us to Hallerstrasse, which was still close to downtown Hannover. We lived in an upstairs apartment in a two-story house. At ground level there was the equivalent of two double garages. This house was located in the back yard of a four-story apartment house with a passageway in the middle, big enough to drive a truck through. All of this suited my father perfectly well. His business was closer to his customers, and he could store some of his goods for a short while in the space downstairs. By now, his business had become exclusively wholesale, with the exception of some rich private homes, mainly doctors. He was selling poultry and game – but no more vegetables – to restaurants, hotels and hospitals. For my father's business there were a couple of times a year when it went really well. The people of northern Germany like to eat rabbits at Easter and geese at Christmas. Families for whom a big goose was too much or too expensive would buy a duck for Christmas. I remember what a treat it was to have smoked goose breast.

However, because at that time there were no freezers like today, at the end of each weekday all the unsold meat had to be taken back to the city's freezer facility. It was located underground, just behind Hannover's main railway station. For this my father had someone with a small truck come to move the meat to and fro. My father often hired a boy to deliver the goods to customers by bicycle. My father had a bicycle built especially for that. It had a small front wheel and above the wheel was a cage two by two feet and little more than one foot deep. At times I got a ride in that cage. From our new location it was only about a five minute walk to get to the freezer.

Looking through my old photo album, I see a picture of my sister and me, completely naked, having fun in a large tub in the backyard. Would this open nakedness in one's backyard be allowed today here in Canada? The picture was taken in the Hallerstrasse in 1935, when my sister was five and I was three. My sister was always a full head taller than I was until I was fourteen; then, within two years, I had become a full head taller than her.

When I was about four years old, I contracted scarlet fever. I still see myself in this hospital room, looking out the second floor window, and seeing my mother walking away, leaving me behind in this strange place with strangers. I held on to my teddy bear and cried. My mother often spoke about how bad she felt about having to leave me there, and the nurses told her how much I cried. It must have also been at that age when I had my first inflammation of the middle ear. It was my left ear that was inflamed. I don't remember any details of this, but my mother told me that the eardrum had to be punctured to let the puss out. I also contracted chickenpox when I was little. After a chicken pox infection, the virus remains dormant in the body's nerve tissues. The immune system keeps the virus at bay, but later in life, usually in an adult, it can be reactivated and cause a different form of the viral infection called shingles. This happened when I was 85 years old; I got the shingles, a very unpleasant condition. I was lucky to have caught it in its early stage; the outbreak was only a couple of days old. When I took medication for it, it only lasted for one more week or so. If shingles are diagnosed only a couple of days later, they can become very severe and it can take months to get rid of them.

I vividly remember one thing that happened in our house in the Hallerstrasse. My best friend had red hair; my father always called him Rotfuchs (red fox). He was a year younger than I was. One day when I was about five, we went into one of the closets in my apartment and examined our genitals. Suddenly, my mother opened the door. I don't remember what was said at that moment; I only remember that my mother was very angry and I was very embarrassed. My friend went home right away, tried to avoid my mother and stayed away from our house for quite a while. I'm not sure whether my mother said anything about this incident to my father. If she did, I don't think it would have bothered him that much. I don't know whether my mother lost any sleep over it either. We never talked about it.

One day my red-haired friend invited me for lunch. His mother was making potato pancakes, and he knew how much I liked them. Even today, I just can't get enough of them. I like them best with lots of white sugar sprinkled over the top. When I was in my twenties, I once had 32 potato pancakes for supper. My friend's family lived at ground level in the four-story apartment house in front of ours. If I remember right, he had at least three other brothers and sisters. When we sat down to eat, I was placed at the end of a long table with my friend on one side and his mother on the other side. I think his father was sitting at the other end of the table. His mother put one big pancake on my plate, and everyone started to eat. I also started eagerly and had already swallowed three or four bites when I realized that these pancakes contained onions. I could eat onions raw like apples, but I couldn't stand cooked onions in my mouth. My mother did not put cooked onions in pancakes, and she was very tolerant. If I didn't want to eat something, I didn't have to. Although my mother would put onions in soups and most other dishes, I was allowed to fish out whatever I didn't like and place it along the rim of my plate. Here, I wasn't at home. So when I suddenly realized that I had eaten onions, I could not help myself. I turned my head to the left and emptied my stomach right onto the floor. Needless to say, that was the only time that I was invited to eat at my friend's place.

I don't know how we managed to live in that apartment, space-wise, and why we sublet one of the upstairs rooms to a young man, Herr Budde. I suppose my parents needed the extra income. Herr Budde only slept there and was gone most of the time, but he always had breakfast at home on Sunday mornings. My mother would make him a peppermint tea and he would make himself thin slices of caraway seed bread with liver sausage spread, sprinkled with pepper. He was a very pleasant young man, and every Sunday morning he would ask me to eat with him. I was a fairly shy boy with strangers, but sharing breakfast with this man was something special. During the week, when it was getting closer to Sunday, I was already thinking of sandwiches with liver-spread and sweet peppermint tea. Many people like to drink tea without sugar. Herr Budde got me hooked on putting sugar into tea, especially peppermint tea.

Once in a while, after Sunday breakfast, Herr Budde invited my sister and me to go for a walk with him. My sister and I would wear black velvet-type suits, something like navy cadet suits, but black. We always walked into the downtown part of Hannover where the large department stores, up to ten floors tall, were located. Herr Budde worked in one of these stores. Some of the girls he worked with must have seen him, and for a while Herr Budde let on that the children were his. He would come home from work on Mondays and tell my mother how much of a kick he got out of leading the girls on. The same Herr Budde came back to see us, but mainly to see my father, a couple of times after the war, almost ten years later, when he wanted to borrow a large amount of money. He was a paratrooper in the German air force during the war. He said that they often had no action and that he spent that time figuring out how to win playing roulette in a casino. Luckily for us he could not talk my father into giving him any money. When he came back the second time, after months had gone by, he said that he won quite a bit. But he still asked for money, which he did not get.

My parents were always busy. They did not have much time for my sister and me. They seldom took us to a park, or even for a walk for that matter. However, my mother did look after us fairly well. Although she worked from perhaps six o'clock in the morning until eleven o'clock at night, she made sure we were well dressed and well fed. We got lots of instructions from our mother, not so much from our father. I didn't go to school yet, unlike my sister. She started school in 1936, two years before I did.

One day I was playing with other kids on the street and climbed up onto a store window sill lined with three-inch upright spikes. The spikes were supposed to stop kids from standing on the sill. I slipped, and my behind slid down the window glass, landing with one rear cheek on one of those spikes. I was on a meat hook. The pain only started a second or two later. I was able to get off the hook all by myself. I then went home crying, hobbling through the passageway of the front apartment house. Besides the application of a bandage, I got a "You must not climb up on window sills like that."

* * *

The other thing that I remember from the time living on Hallerstrasse in 1936-37 was that there was a bakery shop at the corner of our block. When my father was in a good mood and wanted to please me, he would take me to the bakery and buy me a rum ball. This was such a treat for me. The rum ball was about two inches in diameter, not quite the size of a tennis ball. The consistency was like the inside of rye bread, but the taste was something else. It was so *chocolaty, marzipanny (a new word)*, with rum. The outside was covered with chocolate crumbles the size of caraway seeds. My father said that the baker kneaded all the leftovers, even crumbs from the floor, to make these balls. He didn't have to bake them. The crumbs were from baked cake or bread wastes and they were by themselves already edible. My father would kid the baker about some of the ingredients, that there were also crumbs off the floor, but the baker just smiled. At the time I thought my father was just joking about the crumbs off the floor – he was always making fun of things – but maybe he was telling the truth. I still like rum balls today, but for some reason they don't taste quite as good as the ones from that bakery. Maybe other floors are not kept quite as tasty.

It must have been after the schools had closed for the summer in 1937 when my sister, mother and I went on vacation. This was the only time before the war that my mother had a vacation. My father was too dependent on my mother helping him with his business. I think my mother was overworked and a doctor told her that she needed a real rest. My father then agreed that she could take the children for a vacation to Thale, a spa town in the Lower Harz Mountain region. At this place we walked up the valley to see the famous rock formations – a granite table rising vertically 250 metres above the valley on one side, and a rocky point on the other called Roßtrappe, meaning "horse footprint." According to legend, a horse had jumped across the chasm and left a large hoof imprint in the granite rock. These rocks were impressive to a little kid like me. Both my mother and sister later talked about me falling when I tried to climb the rocks, but I don't recall that fall. I was only five.

Once in a while, for years later, my mother would talk about this so-called vacation. We stayed in a two-story private pension or boarding house. The idea was for my mother to relax and not have to do anything. We all three lived in an old-fashioned room. I still have this image in my mind of a typical Victorian-type bedroom, with heavy dark curtains from floor to ceiling. The woman who served us was also the cook and owner of the place. I don't remember what the food tasted like, but my mother said that the woman could not cook. One day my mother asked for some tomato soup. At that time, even at home, every meal had to start with soup served in a deep plate, not a bowl like in North America. My mother was not feeling well, so we ate the meal in our room. However, the soup tasted like the cook had dropped a bar of soap into it. My mother called the lady of the house and told her what the soup tasted like. They got into a big argument, and my mother decided to go back home.

So we left the place a few days earlier than planned. We had gone there by train, so we also went home by train. I don't know whether my mother was able or even tried to call my dad. By the time we got home, it was close to midnight. For some reason my mother did not have a key. My father wasn't home; he was visiting his customers, his restaurants, giving them back ten times the profit he had made on them, my mother always said. He often came home drunk from these outings. My mother noticed that one window on the upper floor was not closed, and she managed to get a friend of theirs to come with a ladder. She climbed through the window and opened the main door to let us in. My father showed up loaded around two o'clock in the morning. The argument that ensued between my parents, and their being mad at each other, somehow lasted for several days.

One day in 1937 I got a big brother. In spite of what people know and remember of the political situation, Germany and Poland had a student exchange program going. That summer German families could participate in a student exchange or just take in a kid or two from Poland. Since my mother could speak perfect German and Polish, she wanted to help the Poles in some small way. After all, her parents were still alive, and living in Poland. This fellow came from Katowice (Kattowitz in German). He was twelve or thirteen, and therefore quite a bit bigger than I was. His name was Walter. As I already mentioned, my parents were busy, so Walter and I spent about two months playing around the neighbourhood. He was a fairly nice fellow, and I always told the boys from farther away that he was my bigger brother. I was sad to see him leave. We lost touch completely when the war broke out.

Otto at Weissekreutzplatz, in 1937
where I played soccer after school

CHAPTER THREE
STARTING SCHOOL

In the spring of 1938, when we were still living on Hallerstrasse, I started school. I believe that kids who were born in the first six months of the year started school in the spring, and the others started in the fall. I was born in March. The custom at that time was to give kids a large Zuckertüte, a cardboard cone filled with sweets, on their first day of school. I guess kids were supposed to look forward to getting this cone, to make this drastic change in their lives easier. One also got a Tornister, a knapsack made of thick leather. It was a rectangular box that kept the books in good condition, and it was easy to find things in. It was such a near-perfect container for school kids, why is it not around anymore? I remember not looking forward to going to school. By this time my sister had already been going for two years and I didn't detect anything good about it. All I knew was that it was a drastic change, and I would have to do a lot of things in school instead of playing with my friends.

My first impression of school was that it was strict. There was no talking nor was any kind of communication between students allowed during class. The classroom had about three-metre ceilings. Every hour on the hour the students had to switch to a different classroom. Each room was set up for a specific subject. The school was a huge three-story brick building. The complex was square and was the size of a small city block. In the front and back of the building was a roughly ten-foot-high wall, making it look more like a jail than a school from the outside. The yard between the walls and the building, on both sides, was the playground for the students. The building was also split in half. The front half was only for girls and the back half was only for boys. The way it was split, girls and boys could never meet inside the school or on the playgrounds. There were doors on each floor between the corridors, but they were always locked. At break time, the boys played in the back yard and the girls played in the front yard. The total number of students was about 320 girls and 320 boys.

The first day going to school was awful. I did not want to go. My mother took me on the first day together with my metre-long sweets-filled Zuckertüte. The school was only a five-to-eight-minute walk from our house, but I felt it went too fast. My mother kept telling me that it was going to be alright. We were introduced to several teachers and after a while all the mothers left to go home. I did not know anyone in my class, and I had never been in such a setting before. The first kindergartens were established in Bavaria in 1780 and spread all over Germany from there. However, I did not know anyone in Hannover who went to one.

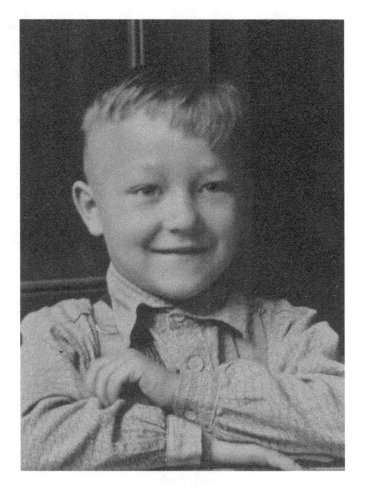

Otto - First Year in School
Standing behind Sandbox

Until age fourteen I was always the smallest boy in all my classes. When I was young I was also a little shy with adults. However, with boys I seemed to make friends easily, even with bigger and often older boys. This perhaps made me physically strong, since I was occasionally wrestling and fighting bigger boys. In school, it did not take too long for me to find some good new friends my age either. One fellow became one of my best friends, but we could only stay in touch on and off until I came to Canada in 1951. That was for 13 years. Because of my moving around a lot in Canada the first few years, we lost touch completely. When visiting Germany in 2006 I went to this friend's house; his son told me that he had died of cancer the year before. I was very disappointed not having made an attempt to see him on one of my earlier visits to the area.

During my first summer school break, in 1938, I got involved in a street fight between two groups of older kids; they were between ten and fourteen years old. One group was from our neighbour-hood and the other from an adjacent neighbourhood. For some reason the adjacent neighbourhood gang disliked the kids in our neighbour-hood and decided to pick a fight. Somehow our kids were warned that they were coming to our district and they also knew what was going to take place. The kids were well prepared. They had picked a day and time when the Mülltonnen (garbage cans made out of heavy sheet metal at the time) were put out for collection. The cans were full of ashes. There was no garbage, no plastic, just ashes generated from all that was burned in the stoves and ovens. In the larger cities in Germany at that time, heating and cooking was generally done with coal.

Each kid, maybe fifteen to twenty in each group, had stuffed their pockets with small paper bags. They filled the bags with ashes from the cans and met at a predetermined location. Then they pelted each other. The aim of our group was to drive the other group back to their district. I did not know beforehand that this was going to happen; however, when I saw it, I could not stand by and watch the group from our neighbourhood get beaten. I was small for my age, but I was a good thrower. We had the street to ourselves; at that time only business people had cars so the streets had no traffic nor parked cars. We pelted each other for about an hour, until the police arrived. All kids escaped through the backyards, and no one was caught. But what a mess we left on the streets. My clothes, hair and shoes were covered with ashes. My mother was not too happy, but I did not receive any special punishment.

My parents were not very strict. Any punishment that had to be given was normally left up to my mother to administer. Although my parents had a Klopp-Peitsche (like a cat o' nine tails, but shorter), the punishment my sister and I received was fairly mild. This strap was perhaps used on us once a year. In my whole childhood, I only got punished with the strap maybe three times, when it was heavy enough for the thongs to leave marks across my thighs.

It was later on in the summer of 1938 when my parents decided to move to Cellerstrasse, a little over a kilometre away from old downtown Hannover. We moved into a five-story brick apartment building. Our apartment was at ground level right behind the street-front store. My father wanted to open a store so he could really be getting into the retail sale of his goods in a bigger way. This new location was on one of the busiest streets in Hannover.

Schmalzes Store in 1938
after move to Cellerstrasse

The street was called Cellerstrasse because it led to the city of Celle, about 50 km away. It was also the main route from Hannover to the central and eastern parts of Germany, including Berlin. I now had to walk one and a half kilometres to get to school on a very busy street. But it did not take long, and I made quite a few friends in this new location. Somehow I was always ready to do mischievous things, the things that adults did not want or would not allow us to do, like smoking, ringing doorbells and then running away, etc.

In a way I liked this new location much better. Our house was only a ten-minute walk from the Eilenriede, a huge wooded area; perhaps 25 km square, that was more like a park than woods. The Eilenriede bordered on the "List", the district of Hannover where I lived, and it was more or less surrounded by houses on all sides, including other districts of Hannover. At one corner of the Eilenriede was also a big zoo. The wooded area had a triangular well-paved road in the middle that was about 10 km long, which saw motorcycle and bicycle races once a year. There were many children's playgrounds, and a few places where retired men could sit and play Skat, a very complicated card game. They sat on smaller tree stumps that were placed around one large stump that served as a table. This was all arranged by the city's parks department. The Eilenriede also had a lot of wildlife, like squirrels, rabbits and deer etc.

I remember going to the Eilenriede with my friends quite often. On the way there was a villa, one of those large pretentious houses, just at the corner before entering the woods. All the houses on the street running along those woods were villas with large iron fences and gates. The villa we had to pass had wild vines growing up one side of it. Somehow we found out that one could take dried twigs from the vine, break them into three inch lengths, and smoke them like cigarettes – these twigs were hollow on the inside. When lit, there was no flame, and very little smoke came off them, but they burned in our throats just like inhaling smoke from wood. I'm sure that it was not a healthy activity, but we would only smoke one per day once in a while when we felt like it. It was perhaps more the adventure involved that made us do it than the enjoyment we got from smoking this wood. We had to risk getting into the grounds to break off a few twigs, and we had to hide smoking them. That in itself is a great adventure for six-year-old kids.

My father was a heavy smoker. He had brown fingers from always having a cigar or a cigarette on the go. At that time, one of the tobacco companies had a coupon collection scheme going. Every time my father bought a package of cigarettes, he would get a coupon. After he had collected enough coupons, he could mail them in and receive an album full of pictures with captions. My father managed to get two albums. I don't know what subjects were available, but my father got one album about the 1936 Olympics held in Germany and one about England. I believe my father only looked at these once when we first received them. He more or less gave them to my sister and me to look at and keep. I looked at them quite often. They were picture books to me.

The Olympic album had pictures of the sports events of the 1936 Games, at which Germany did fairly well. To the Nazis, being healthy and good in sports was something that every German must aspire to. The Aryan race was considered by the Nazis to be the best. Why couldn't sports have been considered to be good just for the sake of keeping one's own body healthy instead of having to think about the whole race?

The second album was about England and the Boer war. It had pictures of the British, only two of which stick in my memory. One was a caricature of Winston Churchill smoking a big cigar. The other picture was a drawing of a railway train with flatbed cars in South Africa. The cars had six posts, one at each corner and one in the middle of each side. Women were tied to these posts with their arms behind them, some half naked. On each flatbed a couple of British soldiers guarded the women with bayoneted rifles. This album was plainly created to instil hatred of the British. Churchill was not even the prime minister at that time. I think my mother, to my regret now, put these albums, as well as my two stamp collecting albums, into the basement after I left Hannover in 1943.

One day, in the fall of 1938, I developed this tremendous earache again. In those days people tried all kinds of home remedies before going to the doctor. If it was something completely new, the neighbours, friends and relatives were asked. I couldn't go to school with this pain and that was usually all right with me, but this pain was worse than school. For a whole day I got these hot camomile packs on my ear, but the pain got worse. On the second day a doctor was called. He had one look and said that the ear behind the eardrum was full of puss and he would have to puncture the eardrum right then and there. I recall lying on the sofa in the kitchen on my back when the doctor put this needle into my right ear and through the eardrum. I was given no local anaesthetic but I didn't feel the needle puncturing. I guess the earache was so overwhelming. A lot of puss ran out of my ear, and the ache lessened. I still got the camomile packs after that, and I think I went back to school in a couple of days.

That brings me to what happened to me in school one day. I think it was my father who had given me a mechanical pencil that he had found and didn't want for himself. For a seven-year-old this was something special; not many kids had mechanical pencils. I was sitting at my desk in school one day when the pencil stopped working. With my urge to investigate and always try to figure out how things worked, I took the pencil apart. I lifted the tube toward the ceiling to see if there was any lead left, when all of a sudden a piece fell into my right eye. I rubbed my eye a little, and because there was no lead in the pencil I put it back together. But there was still something in my eye, so I kept rubbing until the fellows next to me asked me "what is wrong with your eye?" By that time I saw that my right hand was all blue, and I was told that my face was all blue too. The teacher came over and grabbed me by the arm and took me to the office while asking me what I had done. The pencil must have been a Blaustift, a blue pencil widely used by business people because it was not erasable (the ballpoint pen was not yet common). The blue lead would dissolve like ink when it was dampened. I remember my father putting the regular Blaustift pencil to his tongue before he put it to the paper. It always left some blue ink on his tongue. Anyway, I was taken to a hospital where my eye was washed out again and again. After that I got some cream put into my eye and then a black patch was put on. This patch stayed on for about three days. In school I became some sort of special guy, I guess more of a curiosity than a hero.

One day my mother mentioned that one or two kids in the area had contracted diphtheria, and that I should tell her right away if I felt something. In the 1930s, diphtheria outbreaks were quite common. The symptoms are similar to the flu, and in rare cases can cause death. I don't know how she knew what the neighbourhood kids had when I hadn't heard anything yet. I suppose being in our store all day, she spoke to a lot of women and relied on word-of-mouth information. Sure enough, one day I got a strong pain in my throat. Well, in those days, people did not go to the doctor with every little thing, like they do today. My mother told me that I most likely had diphtheria and there was only one thing to do. In America, she said, the kids have to drink some kerosene, and that tastes terrible. In Europe, the old and proven remedy was to drink one's own urine. I first refused, but my mother's insistence, and the threat of dying if I didn't do it, convinced me to do what I was told. She gave me a cup to pee into. I'm not sure if I went into the toilet to pee into the cup. But I remember standing next to the stove in the kitchen and taking a swallow. I gagged and spit into the sink. She urged me to try again. I then actually took a mouthful and swallowed it. After that I refused to do it again and my mother said all right. Surprise, by the end of the next day my throat felt normal. I heard that a girl in our neighbourhood also had a sore throat, but I don't know if she also had to drink her own pee.

Perhaps the best friend I had at the beginning, living on Cellerstrasse, was this fellow Walter. He was a year younger than I was but he was one of those guys who were always full of mischief. His parents owned a tobacco and smoke shop, and once in a while he managed to sneak out a few cigarettes. That was always exciting because we then had to find a place to smoke them. If he had only one cigarette, we would share it. But if he had more, often three or four, we would smoke only one cigarette each and hide the rest. Often we smoked in the Eilenriede woods, and one time we hid some cigarettes there. We only did that once, because we didn't figure on the rain that could come before we got back to retrieve the hidden treasure.

Walter also had a sister, Waltraut, and she was about my age. She often was part of the gang. One time we were in her room in their upstairs apartment, and the parents were downstairs in the store. They lived in a four-story house like I did. Well, we got the idea of playing doctor. Waltraut had to lie down on the floor with her pants down. We did this in the dark and lit matches to see. If one of the parents came up, the darkness might give us time to cover up our activity. We ask her to turn around to lie on her belly. While I was looking at her bum, the match in my hand burnt back far enough to scorch my fingers. I let the match go and it fell right into the crack of Waltraut's bum. She let out a loud scream, jumped up, pulled up her pants and gave us a piece of her mind. Walter and I laughed, but we knew this was no fun for her. This was the first time we did this with her and, needless to say, also the last.

My sister had a bicycle and I didn't. However, I was allowed to use hers, or, better, I took it when she wasn't home. We both had roller skates. These had steel wheels and they really worked well on our paved streets and concrete sidewalks. I was so good on the skates that I could skate as fast as I could run without them and then stop almost on a dime. At times I went to places on my skates that were several kilometres away. The Eilenriede in the city of Hannover had a triangular well-paved road on the inside that was about 10 km long, and it had a walking path running about 100 feet away and parallel with it. This road and walking path led to the Hannover Zoo and various other places that people would stroll or drive to on nice weekend days. It was the perfect surface for me to skate on.

My sister told me about the roller skate rink near the zoo. She had gone there with her girlfriends and enjoyed it very much. I decided to try out this rink for myself. It took me about a half hour on the road through the Eilenriede to get there. The rink looked similar to an ice rink, except the surface consisted of polished marble slabs. They were so well put down that one did not feel the joints between the slabs. I watched the skaters, mainly kids, skating fast and trying to do figures, just like on an ice rink. It looked so easy. If they could do it, so could I. When I finally went onto the rink, I went down on my bum as soon as I wanted to move. It felt like I was on an oiled surface. I'm not a quitter, but after several tries I gave up. I didn't think it was worth the effort to learn how to stay upright on this kind of surface. I then discovered that the figure skaters had skates with wooden rollers. Although there were other kids with steel rollers doing just fine, I was not going to try any more. I didn't go back to that rink until years later, 1951, but not to skate.

My sister, two years older, had many girlfriends. In 1938, at six years old I had my friends, mainly boys, but often there would also be some girls involved. We had all kinds of mischievous ideas. Sometimes my sister's friends became our targets. That would get me into trouble with my taller and older sister. Our parents were always so busy that they often did not know what we were up to. The worst thing I can remember doing was chasing my sister through the apartment with a fire poker until she locked herself in the toilet.

We did not have a bathroom. We only had one toilet, which was in a room the size of a closet. There wasn't even a sink in the toilet, which was next to the kitchen. So, when one wanted to wash one's hands or any other parts of one's body, one had to do that in the kitchen. We had a large tub that had to be brought up from the cellar once a week, for the big weekly bath. Privacy was no problem – when we knew that someone was washing him or herself we just left the kitchen alone. I also think there were locks on the two doors to the kitchen. The main door into the apartment from the big stairway in the building led to a corridor, or hallway, which was ten metres (33 feet) long. From the corridor there were doors to all the rooms except my sister's bedroom. It had a door from the kitchen and one from the living room. I was sleeping in my parent's bedroom.

That brings me to the feeling I always had, namely that my sister always got preferred treatment from my parents. She had a bicycle, her own bedroom, and was allowed to stay up longer in the evening.

Of course, I realized already by the time I was in my teens that we both got equal treatment from our parents. My father hoped that one day I would work in his business. Perhaps that caused him to start the gift-buying for me. Before the war, I had plenty of old toy soldiers, a toy army truck, a toy air force searchlight, a Trix constructor set and an airgun. I'm sure my mother had nothing to do with these gifts, except for the constructor set.

The airgun could shoot lead pellets or darts with tiny hairs at the ends. To catch the lead pellets, I had a heavy steel funnel which had a square frame in the front, into which I could slip cardboard targets. The funnel would be lying horizontally on top of the headboard of my parent's bed, with the target card facing the room. When I shot a pellet from the opposite wall of the bedroom, about 12 feet away, I would always hit the target-card. The pellet would go through the card and get stopped inside the narrow end of the funnel. I seldom took the gun out of the house. But when I did, I would aim, with the definite approval of my friends, at the advertising plate that hung from a bracket in front of the only barbershop in the neighbourhood. This plate was the perfect target. When it got hit, it would make a loud high-pitched ping. The barber would rush out of his store and look for the culprit. My friends and I would hide in doorways and peak around the corners to watch his rage. After a while he figured out that I was the shooter with the airgun, because none of the others had one. My father was a regular customer of this barber. Next time he went to see him, the barber told him about the trouble I caused, and my father promised that when I got home I would receive the appropriate punishment. However, my father thought to himself that's what kids do. So when I came home, instead of scolding me, he made fun of the barber.

However, one time I was standing on the sidewalk in a circle with some other boys when suddenly I was grabbed by the neck and yelled at. When I turned around, it was the barber. He took my gun and went to the police station with it. He said that I used the gun to shoot at a doll that was lying in a girl's doll carriage, which was not true. To make a long story short, my father simply went and brought the gun back from the police.

Not often, perhaps a couple of times, on a Sunday, our parents took my sister and me for a walk through the Eilenriede. We went to the 'Steuerndieb', a large restaurant at one corner of the Eilenriede. The restaurant was about three kilometres through the woods, a good walk to and from. I think that the main reason we went to this place was that this restaurant was a good customer of my fathers. We would get dressed up for these Sunday outings. I looked forward to the pastry, and my father always let us pick out the best. It just struck me how easy- going my parents were when it came to food. My father liked to drink, and every once in a while he would ask me if I wanted to have a taste; it could have been beer or hard liquor. This was standard in most European homes, not that the fathers were drinkers, but that alcohol was never hidden or strictly forbidden for children. I believe it resulted in the children being less tempted to drink alcohol. Even when I was as young as four, when we went to a restaurant my father would ask me if I wanted to drink the foam off his beer. I did, and I liked it. But I only started to have a few drinks on my own when I was sixteen. Smoking, on the other hand, was strictly forbidden, so many kids smoked in secrecy, myself included. Is it not the forbidden fruit that is always tempting? However, I'm not saying that smoking by children should not be forbidden, because it is so much more damaging.

It was only on Sundays that my parents had time to do something special with my sister and me. About two kilometres away, also in the Eilenriede woods, was a fair-sized zoo. I believe my parents only ever took me to this zoo once. It had many different types of animals from all over the world in it. But my mother did not like to go there, she didn't like the smell. I don't understand that to this day. My mother spent a lot of time on farms, and my father's business was not without smells either - there were a lot of animals slaughtered in his business. Maybe she didn't like animal-smell because helping my father in his business was already enough for her?

Only one time in my youth did my parents take my sister and me on an all-day outdoor type of outing. On a Sunday morning, we went to the Listerbad, a bathing facility that was about three quarters of a kilometre long. It was located along the Mittellandkanal, a canal system that was greatly expanded in the 1930s. The canal could take barges from the North Sea all the way to Berlin. The bathing facility was separated from the canal by a cofferdam. Along that dam on the bathing facility side was a six-foot wide catwalk with a railing on the canal side. It was a good place to walk along and watch the barges go by. Sometimes one tugboat would have four or five barges in tow, an arrangement two kilometres long.

The bathing facility was a first class setup. The buildings housed change rooms, locker rooms, shower rooms, toilets and eating facilities. There were four large pools. One was an Olympic-sized pool with a 3, 5 and 10 metre high concrete diving tower. The biggest pool at the other end had a 10 metre high water slide. On a good day there would be several thousand people enjoying the facility. When we were there my parents did not change into any bathing suits. They just sat there on a blanket all day fully clothed. I don't remember seeing any other people there with their clothes on. However, my sister and I had fun.

During the school summer break of 1938, I was about six years old when my sister started going to this bathing facility with her friends. If I wanted to I could go with her; she was my chaperon. We got along well, as long as I did what she wanted me to do, but most of the time what I wanted to do was something else. She already knew how to swim, but I didn't. My sister and her girl-friends liked to jump off the catwalk into the long basin, which was a metre deep on that side – just the right height for my sister and her friends to stand on the floor of the basin with their heads above the water. They swam to the ladder, came up on to the catwalk and then jumped in again. They repeated this to improve their swim-ming. I watched them from the catwalk or gazed at the tugboats and barges on the canal. I could not go play by myself; I had to stay with my sister or the next time I wouldn't be allowed to go with her. One day I thought, I can do that too, and I jumped into the pool like the girls did. Well, what a surprise. I couldn't touch bottom and I couldn't swim either. I splashed around like crazy, swallowing water. A lady nearby noticed that I was in trouble. She quickly came over and lifted me out of the water. I don't recall whether my sister or I told our parents about this incident. If we had, we would have been scolded and most likely I would not have been allowed to go back to the swimming pool. As far as my sister's permission to go to places went, she was often told that she would be allowed to go pro-vided that she took me with her. My sister and I had this symbiotic relationship where both benefited from doing things together.

One day in the fall of 1938, it must have been on Wednesday, November 9, my father told us that we were going downtown into the business area where some fires were burning. It must have been already late, perhaps 9 p.m. Our store I believe closed at six or seven, and we had had our supper. As we got closer to Hannover's main railway station, which was right in the middle of the city, we could hear the commotion created by the SA (Sturmabteilung). The German Storm Troopers or Brown-shirts were smashing the windows of Jewish stores and businesses.

This is a model, displayed at the Hannover City hall, of what the old ancient downtown Centre of Hannover looked like in 1937. The Jewish Synagogue, shown in dark, was located right in the centre. This is where most of the Kristallnacht took place on November 9th 1938 in Hannover. I saw the beautiful Synagogue burn. It was totally destroyed by fire that night.

The streets of the downtown business section were covered with glass. This night became known as Kristallnacht, meaning the night of glass. The attacks were retaliation for the assassination of the

Nazi German diplomat Ernst vom Rath by Herschel Grynszpan, a seventeen-year-old German-born Polish Jew living in Paris. As we went farther, we got closer to a Jewish synagogue that was burning. My father did not seem pleased; some of his customers were Jews, and he was totally against the Hitler regime. It is hard to believe that the crowds just stood by, watching the destruction without trying to intervene. But the German people were constantly told by the Nazi leaders, mainly Joseph Goebbels, the Propaganda Minister, that it was the Jews that caused Germany to lose the First World War. The Jews in general had been hated in European countries for centuries, most likely stemming from the Christian churches' claim that the Jews were responsible for Jesus' death.

The spreading of lies and hatred by governments and oppositions has been going on for thousands of years. This includes the convenient practice of not informing the masses of anything bad or harmful the ruling class is involved in. It also includes making anything good the opposition comes up with look bad. In some countries the only job the opposition has is to oppose the government in whatever it comes up with. In these countries, coalitions are looked at as something bad. A coalition is when two or more parties work together, which will consequently represent a broader section of society. Would that not be for the good of the country? This sophisticated human race sometimes can't see the light and change when it is needed and the solutions often are so obvious.

My Father was not a Party Member

My father was the only business owner in his line of work who was not a party member. The Nazis had such tight control over business that they more or less dictated what and how much business one could do. There were government departments for just about everything. My father's business was controlled by the Eierwirtschaftsverband, the department that controlled the breeding, distributing and selling of wild game, poultry, eggs, butter and cheese, and related products. The department controlled how much a business could grow from year to year by setting quotas on how much a business could buy. That automatically put a limit on how much they could sell. During the Nazi era my father sold only poultry and wild game, as well as eggs. Because he was not a member of the Nazi Party, his business was not allowed to expand like all of his competitors did. His quota was set in the mid-thirties and never changed; this was his punishment for not being a party member. His competitors, on the other hand, grew bigger every year.

I only found out from my mother near the end of the war that my father had helped some of his Jewish customers, they were mostly doctors. In the late thirties he helped them to sell their belongings so that they could leave Germany. My parents, mainly my father, hated the Nazis and what they were doing in Germany. However, my parents never talked about it in front of my sister and me. They did tell us stories about kids who got their parents into trouble by saying things about them. When kids talked about their parents' beliefs or activities that were not considered patriotic, the parent or parents were taken away. In one case, an older girl I vaguely knew went to the police and told them that her father was listening to foreign broadcasts. She did this because she was mad at her parents for some reason. The father was taken away, and I don't know if he ever returned. My mother told me near the end of the war that they, my parents, were more afraid of my saying things than my sister. I guess that must have been because I was two years younger and, in their eyes, did not understand the situation as well as my sister did.

It must have been in the winter of 1938 when my father took us to see his parents, who lived in Wathlingen, about 35 km from Hannover. It was a short distance, but I only went to see these grandparents at their house this once. My grandfather was retired. I don't remember what he had done for a living. The house was like a tiny bungalow. My grandparents seemed to be so old. But, it always appears that way to kids when they are little, until they get older themselves. My father's parents were also small people. To me they were strangers. They wore black, and I remember not wanting to stay at their place overnight, although we did. I don't think I had my teddy bear with me, and maybe that is why I didn't want to sleep there. The only other thing I know about them was that my grandmother died of a heart attack before the war. She was hanging up wash on a line outside their house during the winter. She was standing on a little footstool and just fell down into the snow and died.

I don't remember having ever been asked by my parents to brush my teeth. Brushing teeth was not as convenient then as it is today. The toilet we had was not like today's bathrooms, ours didn't even have a sink. To wash one's hands one went to the kitchen sink. So something happened in 1938 that changed my smile from then on. A bricklayer and his wife, good friends of my father's, were visiting. The bricklayer's wife said to me, "Don't you brush your teeth? They're yellow." From that day on I tried not to show my teeth. I didn't even tell my mother, I was so embarrassed. From then on, whenever I smiled I kept my lips closed. Now I can't even show my teeth when smiling if I wanted to; my whole face wouldn't look right.

In those years, 1938 and 1939, we had a neat way to get dessert that was better tasting than what we got at home. About two-and-half blocks away was the still-to-this-day famous Bahlsenkeksfabrik, a huge biscuit factory. When we were hungry, all we had to do was go to Bahlsen to the back of the factory and ask if they had any scraps. We got a bag full of biscuit pieces of all kinds, some covered with chocolate, others with sugar. It was always a treat. These were normally broken pieces that could not be packaged and sold.

I remember playing with my toy soldiers in the beginning of 1939. Although my father was against the Nazis, the military may have appealed to him, maybe because he was in the army in the First World War. I guess he was still dreaming of the old Kaiser Wilhelm -type Germany. As I said earlier, that is why I wound up with the first names I have. So for Christmas 1938 and my birthday in March 1939 he bought a bunch of toy soldiers and some military trucks and a toy-truck-mounted searchlight, like the military used to search for planes in the sky. My mother on the other hand liked to buy me, what I really wanted, and that was a "Trix Baukasten", a metal constructor set. With it I could build cranes, vehicles and all kinds of gadgets. I always liked to build and figure things out. My father was kind of proud of things that I came up with, but my mother was the one who encouraged me the most. It must have been in her mind, and her secret wish, that I would not go into my father's business and become like him.

One evening, at the beginning of 1939, when I was still only 6 years old, I had set up the soldiers on the floor and took the searchlight and placed it on the side. I turned off the lights in the room and slowly moved the truck-mounted searchlight with the light directed towards the soldiers. As I was doing this, I noticed that the shadows of the soldiers were moving along the wall as I moved the truck. My parents were about to go out, and they were just getting dressed when I called them into the room to watch me making the shadows move. My mother was really impressed and for the next fifty years talked about it.

In order to operate this searchlight, I had to wire it up to a set of batteries. This was my first adventure playing with electrical wiring. Not long after this, I heard my mother say that her electric clothes iron did not work anymore. I begged her to let me have a look at it. When she gave her 'all right' I took the iron apart. I used the tools my mother had – a pair of pliers and a set of screwdrivers. I don't remember my father ever using tools. He had two left hands, according to my mother. When I opened the iron, I immediately figured that the problem with the iron must be the wire that was burned off of one of the terminals. I skinned back the insulation and cleaned the wire, like I had to do with the little wires of my searchlight and constructor set projects. I reconnected the wire under the clothes iron terminal, and when I plugged the iron into the 220-volt outlet, it started to heat up. From then on, my mother and I told everyone that I would become an electrician. I was only six at that time. My father did not take that too seriously; there was plenty of time for me to grow up. However, little did he know about my mother's encouragement.

I, likely similar to most boys, always had an interest in finding out more and more about the girls, what and how it's done, and so on and so on. This subject, we are told now, is on the minds of males more often than anything else. Is it this never-to-be-satisfied drive in males that is responsible for the Homo sapiens' population explosion? One of my friends lent me a book one day; I believe the title was *Rebecca*. At this time, reading was the subject I was least interested in, but my friend said you must read this. It was a fictional story about people living in this small North African town. One of the young girls in the village got pregnant and gave birth. There were no big details about how she got pregnant, but there was a detailed description of how she gave birth. It was so different from the vague idea I had of how babies are born that I had to read this passage over and over again. The girl was tied up, standing with her legs apart and the hands tied to a bar overhead. Having had some science courses since, I'm thinking, should gravity not help giving birth in this position? Most large animals do it standing up.

Around this time, whenever my parents went out, my sister and I would first go to bed in our parent's large bed. After they came back home, hours later, we would switch to our own beds, my sister in her own room and I into a smaller bed still in my parents' bedroom. One time when my sister and I were in my parent's bed I asked my sister if we could play doctor and examine each other, like I had done with my friend Walter and his sister Waltraut. She got mad at me and wasn't going to do any of that. She said she would scream if I didn't behave. I was very disap-pointed, but what could I do? At that time grownups did not talk about sex, the kids had to find out about it the hard way, which is doing things by themselves.

That brings me to a little thought-provoking story that the psychologist Jonathan Haidt and his colleagues have been presenting to many people. The story to consider is this:

> Julie and Mark are brother and sister. They are travelling together in the south of France while on summer vacation from college. One warm night they are staying alone in a cabin near a beach. They

decide that it would be interesting and fun if they tried making love. At least it would be a new experience for each of them. Julie was already taking birth control pills and Mark was to use a condom as well, just to be safe. They both enjoyed making love, but they decide not to do it again. They keep that night as a special secret, which makes them feel even closer to each other.

Was it OK for them to make love? No one got hurt, no inbred child will be borne; they will never do it again, so it will not interfere with future relationships, and because it stays a secret the community cannot be offended. There was nothing else except immense pleasure for these two people. There was no victim. So why do people think there is something wrong with what Julie and Mark did?

During the summer of 1939 I started to go to the Listerbad, the bathing facility, with my friends instead of with my sister. We were very eager to learn how to swim, but each of us had his own idea and preference as to how to improve. As mentioned before, the Listerbad had four pools, the largest took up half the length of the whole facility, perhaps 300 meters long, it was a foot deep at the shallow end and a metre deep at the far end. In front of this, for the whole length of the pool was a six-inch-deep wading pool. Next to the long one was a pool 100 metres in length with a uniform depth of 2 metres. It was ideal for jumping in without hitting the bottom and learning to swim. Swim instructors would take their kids to this pool to teach them. These instructors had long poles that were loosely attached to the person who was taking the lesson by a line at the end. If the student panicked or was in trouble, the instructor could keep him above water and pull him over to the ladder.

We watched sometimes to find out what the instructors were telling their pupils. After we were able to stay above the water and swim a distance of about ten feet, we somehow found it best to improve our swimming by jumping into the deepest pool. It was the first pool near the entrance end of the facility. The pool was also 75 metres long, but had a depth of perhaps 8 metres. This depth was required because it had high diving boards. There was a diving tower at one end. The tower had a 10- metre-high concrete platform, a 5-metre-high concrete platform and two 3-metre springboard platforms on the sides. On either side of the large concrete tower structure there was a 1 metre high springboard. At each corner of the basin and in the middle of the long sides was a ladder to get in and out of the pool. We, for some reason, were always drawn to practice and improve our swimming at one corner of this deep pole, on the side where the diving tower was. We would jump in about six feet from the ladder at first and swim toward the ladder. Every day we would daringly increase the distance to the ladder. Who of us could swim the longest distance? It is amazing how well that competition worked. That summer I became really comfortable in the water. I spent so much time at the facility that I looked more like a dark-coloured boy from Africa than a white person.

CHAPTER FOUR
MY FATHER GETS DRAFTED INTO THE ARMY

It must have been around August 22, 1939 when my father said that there will be war soon. I think it was that evening when my parents wanted to go to the "Welfenplatz" to see some sort of an army parade. The Welfenplatz was a large open rectangular ground in the middle of our part of the city, flanked on one long side by a huge three-story brick army barrack and on the adjacent side by a large three-story police barrack. The ground was about a third of a kilometre long and normally used as an exhibition ground. When a circus came to town, it could easily erect three large circus tents and keep all their trailers etc. on the grounds as well. The name Welfenplatz comes from the Royal Welf family that ruled Hannover and, for a while, England. It was the House of Hannover. My parents left perhaps after 8:00 p.m. and my sister and I stayed home. That night, after about 11 o'clock, our doorbell rang once. My sister and I were not allowed to open the door when we were alone. We had already gone to bed and we were told not to put any lights on, to give the impression that there was no one at home. We saw through the opaque glass panes in our apartment's entrance door that there were two men standing outside in the lit stairwell corridor. We were very scared and kept quiet. When we didn't answer the doorbell, they kept their finger on the button for about five minutes. They then went into the courtyard of the apartment house and directed a couple of powerful flashlights at our windows. Our apartment was called the ground floor level, but it was actually about four feet above ground, so that the window sills on the outside were perhaps seven feet above ground. It was not too easy for someone to climb through a window, especially when it was closed. After about ten minutes the two men left, but my sister and I, we were nine and seven at the time, could not go back to sleep. We just couldn't wait to see our parents. After they had gone to see the parade, my father had to go for a bier at one of his customer's restaurants. They came home around 1 a.m. As soon as my father heard what we had experienced he said "they came to get me for the army."

The next morning at eight o'clock, my parents had already opened their store, two men in uniform arrived to draft my father into the army. They wanted to take him right then and there. My mother and I were at home but my sister had already left for school. So my father said that he would not leave until he had said goodbye to his daughter. They first pointed out that he was supposed to have gone the night before and that he must go with them now. However, my father insisted that he would not leave until he said goodbye to his daughter. The older of the two officers then asked what time my sister would come home from school. My father replied around noon. The same officer then said that he was risking a lot, but that he would report that he had not found my father at home and that he would return at 1:00 p.m. He told my father he had better be there. Needless to say, exactly at 1:00 p.m. the two men came back and my father said goodbye to us and left with a small bag with clothing. The next day, my mother was notified that her husband was stationed in a school compound nearby. The school was hastily set up as a collecting point for the newly conscripted army men.

When we saw him in the schoolyard, the next day, he and all the other draftees had already received their uniforms and whatever else soldiers get when they first enter the army. He had the same rank that he had at the end of the First World War – Obergefreiter – which is 'lance corporal' in the British army, and "private first class" in the American army. He looked funny in uniform, the main reason for that perhaps being because he was only five feet tall. He was not allowed to leave the school grounds. He could not come home with us, although the school was not too far away from where we lived, maybe a ten minute walk. There were guards we had to pass at the gate and we could only see my father in the schoolyard, we were not allowed to go into the building with him. The classrooms in the school had been converted to sleeping facilities for the soldiers.

My father told us that he was going to be a cook again, like in the First World War. Someone took a picture of my parents and me standing in the schoolyard. My mother looks the nicest. I seem to have some rundown dried-up dirt on my left leg and my socks were rolled down to my ankles, as if I had just come from a playground. My father in the uniform looked like he had just come back from the front; it looked like an old uniform without his rank markings. The rank markings, two triangles pointing down, should have been on his left arm.

He showed us a field kitchen that was standing in the yard. He told us that this was the type of cooking equipment he was going to use. It looked like the ideal equipment to cook a German 'Eintopf'. Eintopf is a traditional type of German stew which can consist of a great number of ingredients. The meaning in English is simply 'one pot'. For army cooking, I cannot imagine a better way of feeding a lot of people in the field. The cauldron in the field kitchen looked to be the size of the cauldron our apartment building on Cellerstrasse had in the basement, for the tenants' to heat water and wash their laundry. Nevertheless, my mother made Eintopf at home every once in a while. I liked it then and still do today. What can be cooked together in one pot is only limited by one's imagination.

Otto, Mother & Father, August 24th, 1939
Two days after being drafted into the army

My father must have been shipped out around the 26 of August. The war with Poland started on September 1, 1939 and he was involved right from the beginning. Before he left he had told my mother that he knew that this war was going to happen. Although, my father was already forty-one in 1939, he was drafted into the army just a few days before the beginning of the war. He was considered a soldier with experience, having served in the First World War. It was later on in the war that the younger and also older men were drafted as well. Near the end, even teenagers had to go. We had the radio on all day long to find out what was happening. That war had broken out was only announced on the day it happened. My mother worried not only about my father but also about her parents who were old and lived in Poland. The Soviet Union also entered the war against Poland and attacked Poland from the East on September 17. What one has to wonder about is why England and France did not declare war on the Soviet Union as well. Germany and Russia had conquered and divided Poland equally.

Although Poland was conquered in less than a month, my mother was still very worried about my father and her own parents, who she knew were still alive before the war started. I think the first mail we got from my father was about six weeks later, from somewhere. He wrote that he was in Poland, but his address was the address of his unit only. I guess the military knew where their soldiers were roaming around. The total military losses for the Polish army are not known, but the figures for the German losses, killed, wounded or missing, are 45,000. Of course the German government, who was in total control of the news media, always published the German losses as only some fractions of what they really were, they did not want to discourage, or demoralize the German people.

Our store was closed the day my father was conscripted, and my mother had to get rid of all the goods by herself. We also had some goods in the city's freezer facilities. I don't know how she did it, closing the business all by herself. The store windows were covered with heavy brown manila-type paper on the inside. The store stayed locked from that day on for almost six years, until about three months after the war was over.

My sister and I kept going to school. The only difference in school was that, the first thing we did in the morning was to be informed how successful the German troops were in their conquering the enemy. My mother, of course, had the radio on all day; it was only shut off at bedtime. My mother started to get cheques from the government so we could live. The amount was based on some formula that would only keep my mother and her two children afloat and not in luxury, and on a percentage of the profit my father had made during the year before. My mother said that it was barely enough to get by. I guess my father and his accountant did not report all the money he made during the year to keep the taxes down.

* * *

As soon as the war started, the government began rationing everything. Food, clothing, shoes and whatever else were of importance or in short supply was rationed. The German society suddenly became very efficient and inventive; nothing was wasted. They actually looked back at what people had lived on centuries ago and reintroduced some of these forgotten things. All metals, wood, oil, paper, glass, cloth and clothing etc. became precious. From one day, nothing was thrown away, everything was collected. Germany had no oil to speak of in the ground. So they had to find ways to produce things which were made from oil in some other way.

What Germany had in abundance was coal, although, not the best type of coal. British coal was considered to be much better. Germany managed to make an edible margarine, diesel oil, gasoline, plastics, artificial rubber (neoprene - better than natural rubber) etc. from their coal. The blockade of Germany forced them to make sugar and syrup from sugar beets, coffee from turnips and barley, and herbal teas from all kinds of leaves. The substitute coffee and herbal teas were most likely much healthier than the real stuff. Whatever coffee Germany could get hold of was reserved for the 'Luftwaffen Pilots' to keep them awake. The special treat that Germans got allotted at Christmas time was perhaps an eighth of a pound of coffee, just enough to remind them of what it tasted like. This was what people would then crave for the rest of the year. Germany actually got some oil from the US during the war. It was shipped via Sweden, apparently with everyone's knowledge.

In closing this chapter I will try to provoke some thoughts about water.

Why could similar conservation measures not be made mandatory in peacetime as well? Isn't it mindboggling? Should it not be mandatory to build all cities' water and sewer systems so that the drinking water intake is at the downstream side of the river while the water from the sewage treatment plants is discharged at the upstream side? This way, any city that is not treating its waste water properly will reap the consequences of its own offense. A friend of mine from Serbia told me years ago that the Soviet Union had built such upstream treatment plants. Apparently the plan did not work too well. But isn't it a good idea? Why, with today's technologies at our disposal, should it still be acceptable to poison and kill all other species, when it is the human species that is growing like a cancer, covering every inch of this earth? We treat the air, rivers, lakes and oceans as our sewers. There are more than a dozen species getting wiped out every day, due to our human activities on this earth.

We could not be more selfish then what we already are. The new concern people are starting to talk about is the water supply. They are saying 'the whole world is running out of water'. The world is actually not running out of water, but it is running out of potable water. The same amount of water we have today was there tens of millions of years ago, not more and not less. Whatever struggles we have now because of the demand for and availability of oil will be peanuts when the power struggles really get going about the world's water supplies! Man may be able, at tremendous costs, to produce potable water for himself, but what about all the other species on this earth? How will they survive in, and with, all the waters we have polluted, including the huge oceans? All the oceans' large fish populations have already been 90 percent destroyed. The water experts talk about what we have to do to create water supplies for ourselves. What about the other millions of species on earth? Why don't they count?

CHAPTER FIVE
THE FIRST YEARS OF THE SECOND WORLD WAR

On September 4, 1939, only three days after the war against Poland started, Hannover had its first air raid. However, it consisted only of dropped leaflets. People were wondering what was happening; they had never experienced anything like that. We were asked to collect the leaflets but not to read them, because they were full of lies, and written to weaken the will of the German people. Collecting leaflets was done mainly by older kids, who bundled and then deposited them at a collection site. People were already informed not to waste anything, to collect whatever was no longer needed and to take it to designated collection sites. This was all important and needed to help the war effort.

For my sister and me life went on during the winter of 1939/40 just about as it had before the war. The only thing in school was that we were informed first thing every morning how well the German troops were doing. According to the teachers, the army was always advancing, never in retreat. Some of the teachers we had were really mean. We had a math teacher who would not tolerate any talking in class. If he heard someone, which was normally when he was at the blackboard with his back turned to us, he would snap around and throw his keys at the kid who he thought was the culprit. One time he whipped a shoe off and threw it. I guess being quite rough and tough on the students was acceptable in those days.

I was not too crazy about going to school. Maybe it had something to do with the fact that the kids I played with during the summer, in our area, called the List, did not go to the same school I did. Maybe I should have been transferred to a school in our new neighbourhood when we moved. Perhaps the reason for not transferring me was that it was only just a little over 1 kilometre to walk. Or maybe that the school administrations had other worries to content with than transferring kids around. Although, there was one thing I looked forward to at that time, when going to school – playing soccer after school. Right outside our large school building was a large playground; it was more like a park, called 'Weissekreutzplatz'. It had a big grassy area and a basin with a fountain in the middle. Around the grassy area was a little chain-link fence, but the grass was not for playing soccer on. This playground had a very fine gravel area, this is where five or six of my school comrades and I would go, or better, run to, as soon we came out of the schoolhouse, around 3 o'clock in the afternoon.

The 'Tornisters', the school bags we had were solid rectangular leather knapsacks that we carried on our backs. Two knapsacks were put on the ground some distance apart to create the goals at both ends of what we considered was our soccer field. The Tornisters looked like the knapsack that most soldiers carried in Europe in the nineteenth century. They were almost as solid as a hard suitcase but they really protected the books, much better than the loose bags used today. We would play for an hour or two. Often, in the excitement, we played way past the time when we were expected to be home, around 5 o'clock or so. The groundcover in the area where we played was more like very fine gravel, or more like dusty grey sand. When it was wet we would come home looking a mess. At times, one would slide along the ground a little and scrape and scratch the skin a little. That was all par for the course.

When the war started, many people in Hannover suggested that our city would not be attacked by British planes because of the English connection it had with the Royal family. They thought the House of Hannover still meant something to England, but they were dead wrong. It was after the summer school break started that the second air raid in the Hannover area took place, on May 19, 1940. The first three bombs dropped in our neighbourhood were not that far away from our house. One bomb fell in the middle of a street about one block away. It created a huge crater and damaged the main water and gas lines. The whole street was flooded by the time I went to see it. The fronts of the houses close to the crater were also damaged quite a bit. Glass from windows was on the streets as far as a block away. Another bomb hit an apartment house similar to the one I was living in, and shaved off the corner. It was a five-story house and the corner facing the intersection was cut off from top to bottom, like a corner cut off of a block of cheese. It was a clean cut, right across the corners of all the rooms. Most of them were bedrooms. One could see the rooms from the street as if it was a model house that someone created to show what the furnished rooms would look like. The floors were concrete and therefore still half there. Even the furniture that was along the walls was still standing there. On two of the floors, beds were standing there as if someone just got out of bed. It was quite something to see. People came from all over just out of curiosity.

My friends and I looked for bomb fragments. There was a kind of competition between us to see who could find the largest and oddest loocking fragments. Of course, the government had given instructions to gather all bomb fragments and turn them over; they wanted them for the scrap metal. At first we did not turn over our best-looking or oddest pieces, but as the war went on the novelty had worn off and keeping them was no more fun. When school started again in the fall, in this huge brick and concrete school building, the kids would go down into the basement during air raids. Wherever people lived in Germany, they were warned about the approach of enemy planes by very loud blaring sirens. At the beginning of the war, the warning was a two-minute undulating sound. From the middle of the war on, this was shortened to a one-minute undulating sound. At one point in time, around 1942 they also introduced the 'Vorwarnung' (pre-warning), a twelve-second continuous sound repeated three times. Near the end of the war they introduced an 'akute Luftgefahr' (imminent air raid) signal consisting of two periods of undulating sound lasting eight seconds in total. The eventual all-clear signal was always a continuous high pitch sound for one minute.

Germany had an excellent over-the-radio air-raid warning system, at least in Hannover. We had the antenna of our radio, the 'Volksempfänger,' connected to the lead sheath of the incoming telephone line. At that time, only businesses and the wealthy could afford telephones. Of course, after my father was drafted into the army and my mother had to close the business, our phone was disconnected, but the cable was left in place.

At that time, all telephone and most communication cables were protected on the outside by a lead cover. This cover made the cable waterproof and in general protected it somewhat against physical damage as well. Today, we know that lead should be avoided wherever possible, because of the danger of lead poisoning to all living organisms.

However, the radio also had to be tuned to one special frequency, and over this frequency the German population was kept up to date as to where enemy planes were entering German or German-held territory. The number of planes, the directions they were flying in and what the possible attack targets could be were announced. As long as there were enemy planes over Germany, information was given 24 hours a day about their activities. Also, the regular radio broadcast would give warnings and say which cities had been attacked. Quite often, however, in the case of Hannover the planes seemed to be coming back from an attack on Berlin or Magdeburg, where they were assumed to have dropped their bomb loads. In reality, they had only dropped part of their load and were dropping the rest somewhere else on the way home to England. Hannover was surprised many times by this tactic. Of course, after a while people did not quite trust the announcements that said the planes were most likely empty and just on their way home.

The Nazi news media always drastically understated the Allied air attack casualties and damage, in order not to scare the public too much and keep up our courage. On the other hand, the Allied broadcasts in German, by the BBC and later on also by the American Armed Forces Broadcast 'Stimme Amerikas' (Voice of America), of course overstated the casualties and damage they inflicted to achieve just the opposite effect. Hannover city suffered 125 direct air attacks during which 985,000 bombs were dropped. City records show that 6,782 people were killed and more than 75,400 apartments were totally destroyed. Of the 147,222 dwellings recorded at the end of 1939, only 7,489 (5.2%) were completely undamaged. Ours was one of them. This level of damage was, of course, mild compared to some other cities. In the ten cities with the heaviest losses, there were 479,400 people killed. The seventy most heavily bombed German cities lost more than 750,000 German civilians, averaging more than 10,000 per city. The two heaviest air attacks resulted in the following single day losses; Dresden – the estimates, depending who made them, vary from 35,000 to 360,000 dead, Hamburg between 55,000 and 64,000 dead.

Comparing those losses to those of England, its total losses of civilians over the five-year war due to the German bombing were 60,447 dead, but Germany lost more than 3,384,000 civilians, two thirds of these by the Soviet Army. In 2013, the German government estimated that there were still 100,000 unexploded bombs in Germany. Annually they defuse about 5,500 bombs. To this day, every once in a while a bomb explodes somewhere in Germany and people die or get hurt. Bombs explode because of being hit by an excavator or while bomb disposal people are trying to defuse them. Of all the bombs dropped in WWII, an estimated 15% did not explode. Not that long ago, on May 7th 2017, 50,000 people in Hannover had to be evacuated in order to defuse three unexploded British bombs. As of 2018, about 15 unexploded bombs are still found daily in Germany.

Getting back to the summer of 1940, the apartment house I lived in, like pretty well all houses in Hannover, was a brick- walls-with-wooden-floors type of construction. There were four floors above the ground floor, and the "ground floor" level itself was actually three feet above ground. Before the war, there were typically four apartments on each floor of the house. Later on, these floors were converted to create more apartments. As more and more houses got destroyed by high-explosive and incendiary bombs, those still standing were housing more and more people. On the ground floor of all the houses along our street, which was a main thoroughfare, there were stores facing the street with apartments in the back occupied by the store owners. In all of these houses, one had to go up three or four steps to get into the stores, and another three steps to get from the store into the apartments behind. To get to the building ground floor hallway and the stairwell, one had to climb up about six steps.

This raised elevation would certainly help keep floods out of the ground floors. The other thing it did was to allow rooms in the cellars to have windows at ground level, which would let some light in. Nevertheless, these cellar rooms only had dirt floors and were very damp, which is why they were only used for storage. The main corridor in the cellar had a concrete floor. Each apartment in the building had an assigned cellar room. These rooms were dingy and kind of mouldy smelling. Our cellar room was right underneath our store. The tenants used these rooms to store the coal and wood they needed for heating and cooking. Otherwise they only left stuff down there that they considered useless and no longer needed.

I started a stamp collection before the war broke out, with many stamps from pre-war Germany and all over the world. A few years later, when I did not bother with the collection any more, my mother put my two stamp albums into our cellar. I remember that when I got the stamp collection and the pre-war Olympic and Boer War albums out of the cellar after the war, I found the dampness had totally ruined them. Could those albums have made me a millionaire today? Ah well, that's life, and money is not everything.

When the war broke out, inspectors went through all the houses to figure out where the best places in the cellars were to create air-raid shelters. Most of the cellars in our house, facing the street or the back yard, had windows half above ground level. These windows had window wells in the sidewalk which had grates on top of them. In our house, the space considered best suited as an air-raid shelter was one portion of the cellar corridor where the cellars didn't have windows. The city then went ahead and converted that corridor portion into a room with doors at both ends. It is not that these doors were locked, but when closed they were meant to hold back any debris that could come from the areas leading to and from the shelter. Benches were put into this relatively small shelter space, where maybe forty people could huddle together.

Leading from this shelter room were still some cellar rooms, which belonged to tenants. A couple of these rooms had doors that were not be too well secured, as far as breaking in goes, because they were also escape routes to the buildings next door. In case the building above the basement was bombed and collapsed, or was burning due to incendiary bombs, people could escape through basement spaces into the shelters of the neighbouring houses. Large holes were broken through the foundations leading into the two adjacent houses. These openings were bricked up again, but in such a way that one could, with the use of a hammer, easily break through them. One could, if one had to, go through the cellars from one house to the next, right around the block, until arriving back at one's own house.

Our city block consisted of about twenty four- and five-storey houses. In each house there was one person appointed as 'Luftschutzwart,' air-raid warden. It was always the most able-bodied person in the building. At the beginning of the war, there were still some men who were considered too old to go to the front. These were appointed as wardens. The one thing that people really developed was camaraderie. People really helped each other and looked out for each other.

The air-raid wardens did not have the easiest jobs either. Their duty was to check the condition of the buildings during air attacks. Our house survived the war but it did get hit three times in the first years of the war by incendiary bombs which failed to explode. Our warden disposed of all three of those fire bombs. He went into the attic on three different occasions and found these unexploded incendiaries, which he threw out of the attic windows into the backyard. The incendiaries were fire bombs that had a hexagon shape with a diameter of about three-and-a-half inches and a length of about three feet. The bottom of these bombs consisted of a steel section about ten inches long, weighing 1.7kg. On top of the steel bottom was an aluminium container filled with magnesium and at times phosphorus. The idea of the steel part was to provide lots of weight, so when dropped from several thousand feet, it would puncture a wooden roof and maybe the attic floor underneath. After the bomb hit, a fuse was to cause a small detonation, to burst the aluminium container apart, dispersing and igniting the magnesium or phosphorus. Magnesium burned at a very high temperature and when it hit a surface, it stuck to it like burning glue. At times, magnesium would stick to people, and the only way to stop the burning of limbs was to cut the limbs off. When hot water hit the magnesium, it caused a violent reaction by itself, making things even worse.

The three firebombs which hit our house luckily were duds. They did not ignite and did not go through the attic floor into the apartment below; consequently the warden could easily find them.

The jobs of these wardens were not the kind that one would envy. The wardens were men that were not fit to be drafted into the army. They either were too old, had health problems, or had some other physical shortcomings. Our warden, Hartmann, had a wooden leg. Whenever there was a lull in the bombing they had to go up the equivalent of six floors into the attic to see if a fire bomb had hit. There were buckets of water and containers of sand up there to put out small fires. If they could not handle the problem they had to go and get help from the other people in the shelter or call the fire department. Calling the fire department was OK at the beginning of the war, but as it intensified there weren't enough fire fighters around to look after the city properly. If a warden waited too long to go up and check the attic during an attack, he could easily have been too late to save the building.

There were also wardens in the neighbourhood whose job it was to see that all the windows and doors were properly covered at night so that no light was visible from the outside. It was called 'Verdunkelung' (black-out), meaning darkening. Accidental violation of this Verdunkelung-law was not a crime. The warden would just tell the people in the building to do whatever it took to darken the place. However, frequent violations or refusal to comply would have been considered a crime. Lights visible from the air could help enemy planes to navigate or they could become targets for bomb attacks. Because we lived on the ground floor level, we had shutters on the outside of some of the windows. These may have prevented someone from breaking in but, with the cracks between the boards, they were not tight enough to prevent light in the rooms from being seen from the outside. I don't remember why but our shutters were always left open. We had black roller blinds on the inside of the windows; these we pulled down at night before any light was switched on. Hannover was actually an easy target to find, because it had a big lake, 'Steinhudermeer,' about 30 km west of it. The lake was about 10 km in diameter.

During the war, German cities were pitch-dark. Even the street lights were off. In the beginning, it was kind of eerie to walk around the city at night, especially on a cloudy night or during a new moon, when it was pitch dark. But humans easily adapt to all kinds of conditions. What was done in Germany was that people would get phosphorescent buttons that would glow in the dark. There were also strips glued onto objects that one could run into, like poles, or so that one could find doorways etc. The problem with this phosphorescent material was that it had to be exposed to light first before it would glow in the dark. After exposure it would glow brightly in the dark at the beginning and slowly lose its luminescence. After 45 minutes it would hardly be visible. This phosphorescent paint was also put on the numbers of wrist watch dials and on clocks. Kids had a lot of fun playing with these buttons, trying to see whose luminous button would glow the brightest and longest. We would expose the buttons to light again and again to see if we could beat each other. As the phosphorous paint got older it would also lose its capacity to glow. So it became a game to get new buttons. It was only after the war that the public was told that this type of phosphorous paint actually gave off a small dose of radiation, similar to X-rays. The paint itself, before it dried, was also poisonous. All of a sudden playing with this stuff became a big no-no.

During the raids in the first couple of years of the war, my mother, sister and I were in our cellar bunker with the rest of the tenants of the house. During the first few months there were air-raid alarms but no bombs had fallen on Hannover. These alarms were quite distinctive, but in the beginning they were often ignored. Sometimes the pre-alarm would be in effect for thirty to sixty minutes before the all-out-alarm signal was given, or sometimes the all-out never came. When the first bombs fell in 1940, we were in the cellar. Although the closest bomb hit about a block away, our house shook quite a bit. A lot of dust came down from the ceilings and ledges in the dingy and otherwise never-used cellar rooms. We could not hear the sirens when we were in the cellar shelter, so we relied on the warden to go out once in a while and check if the all-clear signal had been given. The first thing we did was check our own apartment to see if anything had been dislodged. Some things were shifted and we learned how best to arrange things so they would not fall down or break. I believe two window panes were broken when the first bombs fell.

In early 1940 the German government started the 'Welfenbunker' and completed it in 1941. I believe it was the first large air raid bunker of the three that were built in Hannover. It was built to hold 10,000 people. In addition, there were many smaller ones built, some of them perhaps to hold as many as 1,000 people. These bunkers were really needed, because from this point on the bombing steadily increased.

I watched them build the bunker just over a kilometre from our house. The bunker was built on the already-mentioned Welfenplatz (the parade ground). I spent some time there with my friends because there were sand hills to play on. Some hills were of sand for making concrete and others were of the dirt excavated from the hole in the ground, in which the basement level of the bunker was constructed. Some of the sand hills would be thirty feet high or more, a good slope to slide down and also a good observation point to look into the hole and watch the construction. I always came home with sand all over and in my clothing.

The bunker had one floor below ground, one floor at ground level and one floor above that. The outside walls were about four feet thick, made of reinforced concrete. The top ceiling slab protecting the structure below it was about ten feet of reinforced concrete. I can still see the reinforcement steel layers, the steel bars were close together and they were crisscrossing layers, one above the other for the whole ten-foot thickness. When the bunker was finished, it looked like a regular big building. It had a regular roof with terracotta shingles and windows in the attic. The roof was to look like a roof of an ordinary house. The bunker was about 150 feet long and 60 feet wide. It was designed to hold 10,000 people, but during some of the worst attacks it probably contained an extra 3,000 to 5,000 people. From our house it was a ten to twelve minute walk to the bunker, and often, at least for the last year of the war, it was more of a five minute sprint every time.

In the beginning, and until the bunker was built, we went into our cellar during the air raids. I always carried a tiny suitcase, a small cushion and my teddy bear. The teddy was my security blanket. I think I was seven or eight when I knitted a sweater for this guy. He had almost no more fuzz on some parts of his body, but even at that age I just could not go to sleep without him.

CHAPTER SIX
MY FATHER'S MOVEMENTS DURING THE WAR

My father was transferred a few times during the war. He was sent to France three times, for a month or so long before D-day in 1944, and then he was shipped back to the Eastern Front. During these occasions he was able to let my mother know in which city close to Hannover he would be and on what date and time so that she could meet him for an hour or two. I don't know how he did that, our phone was disconnected. There was a butcher across the street and a couple of houses over from us. The owner was a good friend of my father and maybe he phoned him to get my mother on the phone. In my photo album I have pictures that were taken mainly at the railway stations where they met. During the six years of war my father had furlough three times, once for about a week, a second time for two weeks and once in 1944 when he could stop by for a few days while on his way back to the Russian front. In the six years as soldier he spent about 51/2 years on the eastern front. The odds on surviving that were unbelievably slim.

In March 1940 he came home for a few days and then had to go back to his unit in Poland. He told my mother that he had visited her parents who lived in Poland and that they were all right. It was only later, through a letter my mother got from her parents, that she found out that my father had asked them for a couple of pigs. They gave him the pigs but he never paid for them. I gather that he had promised to pay them in some form other than money. He may have had good intentions but he was also not in control as to where and when the army would move him around. But my mother never forgave him for that.

In 1942 my father spent about two months in France. This was another occasion when my mother and I could see him in Osnabrück for an hour. He was on his way back to the Russian front. Osnabrück is about 150 km west of Hannover and we had to go there by train. My sister was already removed from Hannover as part of the 'Kinderland-verschickung,' the evacuation program the government had to ship kids into areas that were considered safe from the Allied bombing.

Otto, mother and father
when he was sent back to the Russian Front in 1942

In March 1943 my mother and I went to Celle to see my father. I have a picture of myself at the railway station; however, I don't recall where my father was coming from or going to this time. The city of Celle is about 50 km away from Hannover and very close to where my father's father and sister lived. I'm not sure whether he was able to see them as well. I doubt it. I guess I was too young to really grasp what it meant to part from him at the end of these visits. I knew it affected my mother more than me. But when one sees a father for only a few hours three or four times in several years, one perhaps does lose some of the closeness.

On June 26th 1943 my mother saw my father briefly in Hildesheim at the railway station when he was on his way to the west. In the picture he carried his belongings, including a blanket, in a Tornister on his back. Hildesheim is located about 40 km south of Hannover and my mother had to go there by train. I wish I could talk to my mother now and find out how my father could communicate with her and let her know where he would be and at what time so they could get together. After all, it was war time and Germany was already doing very badly at this point. I was already, like my sister a year earlier, in 'Kinderlandverschickung'.

On September 5th 1943 my mother saw him briefly at the Hannover railway station when he was on his way back to the Russian front.

March 1944 was the last time we saw our father during the war. He could stop over at home for a few days when he was going back to the Russian front after having spent a couple of months as a guard on tugboats on the Rheine River and its connecting canals, moving equipment about. When he saw how the Allied bombing had already destroyed Hannover and other German cities by then, he said that it was probably safer to be at the front than in a German city. He was with us just before my sister Hannelore finished primary school at the age of 14, and then had her confirmation in the church. However, he had to leave just a couple of days before these things took place. That was tough on my sister. From that point on, my mother got only a letter or two from him. For nearly a year, up until July 1945, we did not know whether my father was still alive or not. The Russian front at that time was just one big chaos for the German army.

But it was early in 1941, perhaps January or February, when my father really created trouble for himself. Long after the campaign against Poland was over, my father was given two weeks leave, to see his family. The purpose of this leave must have been to raise the spirits of the German soldiers before the invasion of the Soviet Union. Of course my father did not know that it was exactly this invasion that was awaiting him when he got back to his unit. Not too many Germans imagined that Germany would attack Russia. The two countries had a nonaggression pact between them and both attacked and shared the territory of Poland equally. England and France declared war on Germany because it had invaded Poland. What about Russia? It had invaded Poland at about the same time and occupied the other half of it. Was that not also a war crime? Why did they not also declare war on Russia?

The type of man my father was, he had to have a party when he came home. My mother did not have anything to put out for a party. But my father was always able to make deals when he put his mind to it. One has to consider that at this point Germany already had strict rationing and everything was in short supply. Nevertheless, with whatever he could lay his hands on; he was able to get some drinks and food together. To that party he invited a bunch of ladies – he always was a ladies man. However, these ladies were the wives of officers from his army outfit. In addition, he invited one other young soldier from his outfit, a fellow that had come home to Hannover with him. I remember this evening so well because my mother talked about it again and again. The young soldier played with my sister and I and spent just about all his time with us. As he often did, my father tried to entertain and impress people, especially when he had had some drinks. He was telling the ladies stories about the war. In doing so, he was also telling them how terribly the Poles were being treated by the Germans at times. I remember only that he had a picture of a Polish prisoner of war who was tied to a post. This prisoner was supposed to have stolen a slice of bread from his fellow prisoners and was consequently shot for it.

As soon as my father got back to his unit in Poland he was arrested and accused of spreading lies about the conduct of the German army. He found out that the officers' wives who were at his party had written to their husbands in Poland, asking them if what my father had told them was true. Consequently he had to appear in front of a military court. The young soldier he had brought to our house testified that he had heard nothing of what my father had said, because he had spent all the time during that evening playing with my sister and me. So my father was court marshalled and was sentenced to six months jail in the Fortress of 'Torgau'. This fortress was very old and was now used to house German military prisoners in its very cold and dingy casemates. The term refers to vaulted chambers in old fortresses. My father said that they were beaten on their feet every morning before breakfast I believe. The food they got was also not that good.

By the time the war against the Soviet Union broke out, in June 1941, my father had already served three months in this awful prison. He and the other prisoners were then taken out of that fortress prison and were told that they would have to rehabilitate themselves by fighting the Russians. When they got to the front, they became members of a special squadron. This squadron was issued rifles and ammunition and ordered to attack the Russian forces. As they went forward and were pinned down by the Russian fire, they quickly found out that whenever they tried to retreat they were shot at from behind as well. So they had the Russians in front of them and German SS troops behind, who would shoot at them if they wanted to fall back. Most of his buddies, 80 percent, did not survive this arrangement. My father was lucky again. After three months, the length of his remaining sentence, he was transferred back to his original regiment.

CHAPTER SEVEN
MY SISTER LEAVES HANNOVER – I JOIN THE JUNGVOLK

As the bombing of German cities increased, the German government decided to remove German children from the cities and put them into places that looked safer for them. In the beginning, mainly mothers with preschool kids were moved. However, near the end of 1941 they started to remove primary-school kids, between the ages of 10 and 14, without their mothers. This child-evacuation program became massive from 1941 on. Estimates are that over 2 million children were taken out of the cities. It was called 'Kinderlandverschickung.' I like the way the German language can put words together that would otherwise take a whole sentence. The meaning of that big word is; 'the children's evacuation into the countryside.' They were taking more and more school-age kids from the larger cities as time went on. After my sister left, I told my mother that I wanted to go too, but she said that I was still too young.

In early 1942, when my sister was twelve, she and her schoolmates were sent to Altenau, a small town in the Harz Mountains, about 120 km southeast of Hannover. They were placed in private homes there. The town of Altenau in the Harz Mountains was a tourist-resort type of place. In addition to the hotels, there were individual private houses that the government ordered to take in these ten-to-fourteen-year-old girls. The owners of the houses had to empty one or two rooms in which beds and lockers would be installed. I assume the owners got compensated for this. The girls would eat with their host families and would go to school there, just like they were doing at home.

I remember being at a less lively home now; it was just my mother and I. My mother did not have to spend any time working in my father's store like she did before the war. However, because of the scarcity of just about everything, she seemed to be just as busy. She was doing a lot of sewing, knitting and fixing things. One time I brought home a piece of paper for my mother to sign. It was a paper that showed my latest school marks for all my subjects. The worst mark was for reading. I liked math, but I really didn't like any of the other subjects. My mother got fairly angry with me and in order to help me she started having reading lessons with me. I had to spend perhaps a half hour reading out of a book every day for a short while. I hated that. I'm not sure what the reason was for my loathing of reading. It is possible that it was due to my parents always being busy before the war started. With their business, my mother in the store, and my father on the road most of the time, they didn't have much time for my sister and me. However I kept telling my mother that I also wanted to leave Hannover and go to a place like my sister did. But, my mother always said that I was too young, unlike my sister who was two years older.

1942 was the year I became ten years old. At the age of ten, the German kids, boys and girls, had to join the 'Jungvolk' (youth folks); it was sort of like the boy scouts. My sister had joined in 1940; it was mandatory, like going to school. At the age of 14, kids then had to join the 'Hitler-jugend' (Hitler youth). It was one step up from the Jungvolk. In the Jungvolk, one did not have to have a perfect uniform. These uniforms consisted of dark short or long pants with a special Jungvolk leather belt and belt buckle, a white shirt and a black tie that was worn around the neck and held in place by a woven leather slip-knot. This knot was easy to put on; one did not have to tie a knot with the tie itself, just slip on the knot. My mother didn't want to spend any money on this uniform and she didn't have much to spend either. So all she bought was the belt with a buckle and a knot. When my father was conscripted into the army, my mother got an allowance to live on. This allowance depended on the amount of profit that my father made before he was drafted and how many children my mother had to look after. My mother always said that the allowance she received was unfairly calculated. It was because my father, as a businessman, had not joined the NSDAP, the Nationalsozialistische Deutsche Arbeiterpartei (National Socialistic German Workers Party) that his business was limited, it could not grow. To keep his taxes low he may not have declared all his profit either. So, my uniform was made up of clothes which my mother had sown together, it had colours not perfectly matching what a bought uniform would look like. In the Hitlerjugend, the 14-to-18-year-olds, one's uniform had to be just about perfect.

Our Jungvolk group had to meet every Thursday evening from 6:00 p.m. to 8:00 p.m. There was no way one could show up late; they were stricter with their orders and rules than what I had experienced at school. We often met at some playground in the Eilenriede, the huge wooded park that was nearby. There we played a lot of games, like splitting up into a small and a larger group, the smaller group taking off to hide and the larger group coming fifteen minutes later to find them. It was like finding the enemy. This was done once in a while, maybe once a month, summer and winter. We also played a lot of sports. Fitness was important. Nobody was to become a sissy. When we played sports, it was always done competitively. There were points given for the various sports. Relatively, the highest number of points one could get were for throwing balls. I guess this was considered useful when entering the army a few years later; one would be able to throw the hand grenades farther. The balls were like a baseball. For some reason I was good at throwing, which made up a lot for not being able to run as fast, or jump as far, as the best. At age ten I could throw the ball 80m (265 feet). During these meetings we also heard reports about where the German army was advancing.

On Saturdays we sometimes had to meet and go into the woods and gather leaves from certain types of trees, for making herbal teas. Germany had no access to coffee. The whole of Europe was blockaded so that no goods were coming through to Germany. So, there was no real coffee and no black or green tea. People made a coffee substitute out of Steckrüben (turnips). They would cut them into half-inch cubes, roast them and then grind them up into a ground coffee kind of consistency. This made a brown coffee-like liquid, into which one put a knife-tip amount of thick chicory, to give it a better taste. But just about everyone liked the herb teas; these were actually good for some mild ailments, like upset stomach and colds etc.

For some reason I did not enjoy these Jungvolk meetings all that much. One day I decided not to go to one of them. I forgot whatever else I did that evening, but I assume that my mother thought I was at this meeting. For the meeting the following week I had to have a written excuse from someone for missing. My mother did not know what I was doing the week before so I was not going to ask her to make up an excuse. I did not think it was that big a deal. So I made up a short written note that I was sick the week before and wrote it as if my mother had written it. I also signed it using her name. I was only ten years old. It never occurred to me that the handwriting would give me away. It was on the next Thursday evening that I had to report to the youth meeting. When the leader, an eighteen-year-old 'Hitlerjugend Führer', asked me where I was the previous week, I gave him my handwritten excuse. He took it and the evening went on like it normally did. The more time that went by the more relieved I felt.

However, right after he had discharged the group – we were about thirty to forty ten-year-old boys – he called me over. Well I figured right away that it was about the piece of paper I gave him. He then gave me his home address on a piece of paper and told me to come and see him the next evening at seven o'clock. I just told my mother the next day that I had to go and see my Jungvolk leader at 7:00 p.m., I didn't tell her why. The place was only a ten- or fifteen-minute walk from our house.

When I arrived at the leader's place, he invited me into his apartment. I'm sure he still lived with his parents. He took me into the living room; it was a much better place than what my parents had. His parents must have belonged to the better class in society; judging by the houses, the whole district was of the better class. There didn't seem to be anyone else in this house. We were both standing when he asked me as to who wrote the note I gave him. I very timidly replied that I had written the note, to which he replied 'your mother did not write this?' I said 'no.' He asked me if my mother knew about the note. I again replied 'no.' He then asked me why I did not show up for that meeting. He was very stern through-out his questioning and by this time I was really scared. I told him what it was that I did that evening, with my voice quivering and tears coming down my cheeks. I have since forgotten what it was I was doing, but I'm sure it was something like playing with my other friends. He then told me that this was a very serious offence that I had committed. He told me that it would be my mother that would be held responsible for what I did, and if it ever happened again, she could be jailed.

When I got home, I told my mother the whole story. She scolded me a little bit, but she also spent a lot of time explaining how serious it was what I had done. She told me that kids had had their parents taken away, sometimes over minor things like this.

That summer, during school break, my mother and I were also invited to visit my uncle and aunt Winterberg. Mr. Winterberg was actually the younger brother of my father's mother. So they were not really my uncle and aunt, but my sister and I were told to call them that instead of 'grand' uncle and aunt. They were very religious, and the uncle was a kind of preacher or part-time preacher. They were much older than my parents. My father did not get together with them too often, yet my mother somehow liked them, and in 1942 we visited them fairly often. They lived in Limmer, a suburb of Hannover, about five kilometres away from us. It would take us maybe forty-five minutes by streetcar to get there. They, like many city dwellers in Hannover, had a small flower and vegetable garden. It was about 150 by 200 feet with a large grassy area, some fruit trees and a 'Gartenlaube,' a small summer house. There was always lots of work to be done in the garden. So the Winterbergs would ask my mother if she wanted to help with some of the garden work.

Since she always liked garden work, and she had nothing else urgent to do, she loved the idea. She was always assured that she would bring home some vegetables and fruit later.

The trouble I had was that I did not like the Winterbergs that much. They were too stiff and formal. But my mother could not leave me alone all day, there were also the bombings, although in 1942 they were not yet as often, nor were the raids as heavy. So what was I going to do there all day? I didn't want to go to the garden with them, but for my mother the garden was pretty well the main reason. So I bought myself a piece of thin plywood and some other soft wood, I was going to build a sailboat. Next door to our store, which was closed during all the war years, was a stationary store. The owner operated it with his sister; both were elderly and never married. This stationary store sold also toys and all kinds of hobby and handicraft materials and kits. So that's where I bought my small fretsaw and blades, glue and whatever I needed to do my hobby work.

When we got to the Winterbergs in the morning, we first got some herb tea and a little piece of cake. Uncle Winterberg would then tell my mother what the schedule was for the day. However, my mother and I already knew what that schedule was going to be before we left our home. So I then said to my mother that I didn't want to go to their garden, I wanted to stay in the house and build a sailboat. My mother knew that already, we had talked about that at home. She said that she was quite happy with that. However, my so-called uncle then said that under no circumstances could I be left alone in the house all day. They also lived in an apartment house on the third floor. However, my mother did quite a bit of talking to the uncle to convince him that I would be all right and that they didn't have to worry about anything. The district where they lived was still more on the outskirts of Hannover, which is not the case anymore today. The chance that bombs would fall in that area was a lot less likely than falling closer to the city centre. Anyway, he finally agreed, although very reluctantly, to let me stay behind. I can still today in my mind see the unhappy face he had when they left.

I'm sure he expected me to turn their house upside down before their return home. I on the other hand was now in seventh heaven. I had all the material that I needed to work on my fifteen-inch-long sailboat. I had already done a little bit of the work at home. It was one of these old square-riggers.

When I was finished with all the woodwork, the hull and masts etc., I cut the sails out of material that I had brought with me. But the material was kind of soft and did not hang properly. So I looked around the kitchen and found flour in one of the cupboards. I took some flour and mixed it with water to make a sort of paste. I then took the sails and worked this paste onto the sailcloth. Then I put them on the window sill in the sun to dry. I bend them so that when they were dry they would have the proper shape. By the time my mother, uncle and aunt came back home from the garden in the late afternoon, my sails were dry and in place on the boat. Well, my uncle was so surprised that the house was not a mess and nothing was broken. The first thing he did was go through all the rooms of the house. When he came back into the kitchen, where I was, I could see in his eyes how relieved he was. From then on, I had no trouble staying at the apartment during our visits when they and my mother went to the garden to plant or harvest something.

Hannover, located in northern Germany, does have a climate somewhat similar to England's. In winter it is mainly wet-cold, not a real winter with snow and a dry cold. The one time when it was different was in the winter of 1942-43. That was the coldest winter I had experienced in my childhood, and in addition there was lots of snow. Once one got used to the cold, it was actually fun to play in the snow. There are no hills in Hannover, but the city created a hill in the Eilenriede where they dumped a lot of snow that they had removed from the city streets. There was for the first time a fair size hill to slide down. I had a small sleigh that I could use for several months during this cold winter.

But that was also the harshest winter for the rest of Europe and the Soviet Union as well. It was the winter during which the German 6th army got encircled at Stalingrad and eventually destroyed. The Battle of Stalingrad (August 23rd 1942 – February 2nd, 1943) was the major confrontation of the Second World War; Germany and its allies fought the Soviet Union for control of the city of Stalingrad (now Volgograd) in Southern Russia. In the battle over that city, the German side's losses were more than 800,000 dead and 91,000 prisoners, while the Russians lost 1,100,000. I believe 90 percent of these German prisoners did not survive the Siberian prisons. What a waste.

My father was on the eastern front and he was never allowed to let us know exactly where he was. Luckily he was not in Stalingrad, but my mother found out only a month later that he was still all right. The mail, to and from the front, was often weeks or even months in transit. One could always tell by the date when it was written.

By the way, it was also the Russian winter of 1812 that brought Napoleon to his knees. That campaign effectively ended on December 14, 1812, not quite six months from its outset, with the last French troops leaving Russian soil. It was the greatest and bloodiest of the

Napoleonic campaigns, involving more than 1.5 million soldiers, with over 500,000 French and 400,000 Russian casualties.

Among the friends I had were two brothers who were about two and three years older than I was. They were a lot taller too. They lived only a half-block away from my house so we got together quite often. I felt like these two guys were like older brothers to me. According to pictures I have standing beside them; they were a whole head taller. In the same house where they lived was also a boy who was crippled. His legs were not straight; he could not walk properly and needed crutches. The brothers really looked after this fellow. They would make an extra effort to help him and play with him. The apartment that the crippled boy lived in was located in the back of a larger house. It was a similar setup to the house I had lived in on Hallerstrasse a few years earlier. To get to his place, the brothers had to go through a large doorway-type passage in the front house. While coming back from our bunker after the air-raids, we always had to pass by this place. One day, the four-story front house was bombed out. It was mainly a pile of rubble. Some walls were still standing up to the first floor. A large portion of the rubble was covering our street. In order to get to our house we had to climb over the rubble. It is amazing how fast the city managed to clear rubble, repair the electric power grid, repair the broken underground gas and water lines and replace broken window panes.

Hannover already had a gas distribution system long before the Second World War. This gas was meant for cooking and all apartment buildings throughout the city of half-a-million people were supplied from this gas line. About a kilometre from the centre of the city was a huge storage tank, perhaps 300 feet in diameter and 100 feet tall. This tank was inside a large steel structure that allowed it to rise and fall in accordance with the pressure that was in the tank. When the pressure was high the tank was just about completely visible; when the pressure was very low it was mostly below ground level. This City gas-plant was the first gas-plant on the European continent, it was built in 1826. It extracted gas from coal. At the beginning it was to light up streets and squares using gas-lights on poles. Later it became a gas supply for cooking stoves to just about all houses in Hannover. The area around the tank was comparatively huge and had a wall around it. One could not see what it contained. This tank was visible from a lot of places in the city and it is still puzzling that it never got bombed. The underground gas distribution lines in the streets were often hit; however the repairs would only take a day or two.

During the war, the coal and wood people in our district needed for heating was often dumped onto the grounds in a nearby school-yard. One had to go there in order to cart home one's rations. Before the war and in its early days coal was brought to the house. Our coal was dumped through the sidewalk basement window into our cellar.

It was days after my friend's house was destroyed, when I went to get our ration of coal and wood that I met one of the brothers. We talked about the air-raid and how their front house got hit. I then found out that the crippled boy was kind of slow leaving his place when the air-raid happened. He got caught in the passageway underneath the front house. When the house was hit and collapsed he was squished against one of the walls in the passage. My friend said he was flattened. I was only ten at the time. I visualized this fate all too clearly, and had a hard time getting rid of it. Especially at bedtime, just before falling asleep, the picture would come back again and again.

CHAPTER EIGHT
I'm Shipped Out to a Youth Camp

Sometime in March 1943, it must have been after we saw my father in Celle, all the boys in school got a letter from their teachers that they had to pass on to their mothers. This letter told my mother that I, together with my class and three other classes from my school, was to leave Hannover on a certain date. Not much time was given. I finally became a candidate for the Kinderlandverschickung. My mother had no choice; she had to let me go to this, for us totally unknown, place in the Harz Mountain. At this point I was no longer sure whether leaving my mother was all that great an idea. My mother told me that I could not take my teddy with me. That was something I had never considered until that point. My mother assured me that this move would be good for me and that we had no choice. About the teddy, I didn't want to look like a sissy in front of the others either. So a few days later my mother took me and my little suitcase to the railway station where we met all the other kids. We were about 160 boys between ages ten and fourteen. There were four classes of about forty kids per class, grades five, six, seven and eight, of the primary school I went to. There were a lot tears before and after the train pulled out of the station.

The train took a couple of hours or so to get to Goslar, a small city just at the northern fringes of the Harz Mountains. This being an old historic place, we had a little tour before going on. There was an old castle that we visited. It was kind of fun walking around in this old historical town.

Johanneser Kurhaus in Harz Mountains in 1939, aerial view

Johanneser Kurhaus in Harz Mountains 1943, frontal view

From there we went on by train and finally reached Clausthal-Zellerfeld, an old mountain mining city, about 100 km south-east of Hannover. At the railway station, we were put onto buses to travel another three kilometres to get to our final destination, the Johanneser Kurhaus, where I was supposed to be staying until the end of the war. It lies 600 metres (2,000 feet) above sea-level. When we left Hannover, the weather was quite mild, always above freezing. However, here in the Harz Mountains, it was cold and there was lots of snow on the ground. A few days later we were given a postcard each which we had to send to our mothers, to let them know that we had arrived well. The mail we send was reviewed before it was mailed. My message was brief but good considering I was only eleven at that point. It said *'Dear Mother! I arrived well in Clausthal. We walked around in Goslar and did siteseeing. The toilets are still broken, but we have a 'Donnerbalken', just like the soldiers. The food is very good. The stamp is my address. I send you the best greetings.'*

The Johanneser Kurhaus was a health resort mansion before the war. It was just about perfect for what it was supposed to be used for now. There were two main buildings, the one in which the 160 kids stayed, and an adjacent building about half the size, where the adults stayed. The adults were four male teachers, one per class, together with their wives, as well as a nurse. In addition there were the kitchen staff, cooks and servants etc., all women in their forties. I guess these male teachers were too old for military service at this stage of the war, 1943. Near the end of the war age was no excuse for not getting drafted. As long as a man was physically able to carry a gun, or 'Panzerfaust', an antitank weapon, he was drafted. My guess is that these teachers eventually had to go too. I recollect that my teacher also carried a Nazi membership button on his lapel, that membership probably also helped him to stay out of the army for a while longer. There were also four boys, about seventeen years old, who had to keep us busy when we were not in school. These seventeen-year-olds appeared to us like young adults. They were on the tall side, and not without reason. One of the teachers was the 'Lagerführer', the camp manager. He was the top guy in camp. He also happened to be the teacher of my class. He was tough. The best-looking person was a nurse, about nineteen or twenty years old. She was responsible for our health. The whole place was run as if we were in the army.

The building was not quite ready for us when we arrived. There were quite a few changes that had to be made. Our building had huge rooms at ground level, which I guess were originally used as dining rooms. The ceilings were at least eighteen feet from the floor. Above the ground floor were two floors with rooms. There were perhaps twenty rooms per floor. Three other boys from my class and I were assigned to a room on the second floor. There was a wide staircase in the middle of the building. As one went up the stairs, there were big landings with corridors going off to the right and left on each floor. My room was the third door on the right side of the corridor; its window looked out the back of the building, which was facing the woods. On the outside of the building, over the same length as the five rooms, was a balcony. Being on the second floor, we had a good view over the back of the whole area.

At Johanneser Kurhaus in 1943.
From left to right Rolf-Otto-friend

However, among the things which didn't work yet, were the toilets. For the first two weeks, whenever we had to go for a pee we had to go into the woods in the back of the resort grounds. This was no big problem. However, when we had to do the big one we had to go quite a ways away from the grounds, perhaps 300 feet. There was what we called a "Donnerbalken." It consisted of a trench about forty feet long, having a log along the front to sit on, or better to hang the rear-end over, and a log in the back to lean against. A good 'Donnerbalken' translation could be 'thunder log'. In the German language, often, one or more words are put together to make a new, fairly descriptive word. This may in some cases be instead of a long sentence. In this case, 'Donner' means thunder and the second half of the word the 'balken' means log. Isn't that a good description for such an arrangement? At times one actually could hear one's own or someone else's thunder. Where this arrangement became a little troublesome was at night. One has to imagine a boy of eleven, or ten in the case of the youngest class, waking up at two or three o'clock in the morning and having to do the big one.

Johanneser Kurhaus in 1943. Kneeling, from left to right, Otto, Rolf. Other friends standing.

I wore a white nightgown, like most people who I knew in Germany did at that time. Whenever I had to go during the night, I would speak in a whisper, trying to find out if anyone else wanted to come down to the Donnerbalken with me. I would then quietly climb out of my upper bunk bed. Most of the time, nobody would come with me. We were told not to disturb others. So no lights were put on. The corridors and stairways were lit by red nightlights so that one was able to find one's way around. As I mentioned before, the whole of Germany was under a blackout curfew for the duration of the war, and these red lights were not too visible from a distance. So I put some clothes and shoes on to go down into the woods. It was still cold at this location and there was plenty of snow on the ground. Spring had not come yet. If I had to go down for a pee I did not have to go too far, I just went to the closest tree off the compound. But often I had to go for the big one, also called 'number two'.

So for the two weeks, until the toilets were fixed, I had to follow this snowy footpath to the Donnerbalken. At times, especially when it was cloudy, it was pitch dark and kind of eerie. There would be all kinds of noises coming out of the woods. It could be a bird that I disturbed, or some other animal or even the wind. I always tried to get my business over with quickly and get back to the building as fast as possible. The Donnerbalken was a trench that always had its contents covered with quicklime to disinfect and prevent the feces' smell. But the lime also created a smell that wasn't too pleasant either.

I was always the smallest kid in school and I was not the best student either, but when we were assigned to our room I was given the position of 'Stubenführer', room leader. One boy in our room was actually a whole head taller than I was. It became my job to report on the room's condition, to make sure that it was kept clean and to make sure that it was ready for inspection every morning and afternoon. This was done on a daily basis. We were four boys assigned to one room, and we had to decide between us who slept in which bed. The only things in the room were two double steel bunks, one on top of the other, four steel lockers and two chairs.

We had one fellow in our room who was considered a little bit of a sissy by the others in the class. However, there was never any bullying between the boys, it was not tolerated, whereas punishment by adults was tolerated. This boy also had trouble going to the toilet at night. Every once in a while he would pee his bed. I kept telling him to wake me and I would go with him to do his business, but he seldom did.

However, we were very protective and helped him whenever possible. The mattresses were jute sacks filled with straw, so it was not that hard to fix a soiled mattress. The first few times, before getting a new mattress we would just dry his on the balcony. When it started to smell too strong we would replace it. On the beds were white bed sheets, one covering the mattress and one under the blankets. Each bed had two blankets and one down-filled pillow. The beds were arranged right and left of the room entrance. At the ends of the beds were the lockers with their doors facing away from the beds, towards the balcony side. Most kids preferred the lower bunks, in case they fell out of bed. I took the upper bunk to the left of the room and told the sissy to take the bunk below me. I wasn't afraid to fall out of bed, but I was afraid to get peed on. If someone opened the door, my bed would be the first thing one saw on the left side.

The activities we had every day were planned far in advance and we were more or less told the day before what was going to happen the next day. However, there were a lot of routines that were the same every day. As already mentioned, the camp was run like a military organization. But that was probably the best way to run such a youth camp. Every morning at six o'clock sharp there would be a bugler trumpeting at the entrance of the corridor. It was the signal to get up. The sound was loud enough that there was no chance that one could not hear it. The schedule we had to follow was also so tight that no one could afford to stay in bed an extra minute. Hearing the bugler, we would get out of bed to get washed. The washing facilities were set up on the landings on each floor near the stairway. There was a basin made up of galvanized sheet-metal sheets soldered together. It was like a table, sloped down in the centre, with a three-inch-high sheet-metal boarder all around to prevent water from running onto the floor. The basin was about ten feet long, allowing about a dozen boys to wash at the same time. In our wing there were about forty boys, twenty on each side. They were all from my class. So when the wake-up signal came, the kids from one side of the floor went to wash first, while the kids on the other side started to clean their rooms and then washed fifteen minutes later. It was our side that had to wash first.

Johanneser Kurhaus in 1943.
From left to right: Otto, Rolf, other roommates

By about 6:50 a.m. our room had to be ready for inspection. There was a loud command given at the entrance of the corridor that the room inspections would commence. The seventeen-year-old youth leader for our class would then start at the corridor entrance on our side, because we were the first ones to wash, to inspect the rooms. All the room doors in our wing had to be open. The boys would be standing at attention in front of their beds, two on each side near the door. I, as the room leader, was the closest to the door. The fellow that slept below me would be standing on my left. As mentioned already, our room was in the middle of the length of the corridor. As soon as the leader appeared in the doorway I would raise my right arm to salute and bellow out 'Heil Hitler, Zimmer vierundzwanzig fertig zur Abnahme.' Translated it means - hail Hitler, room twenty-four ready for inspection." I'm not sure about the room number, but the wording of what I had to say is very close. We were instructed, how exactly we had to report to the leader for these inspections.

I don't remember whether the leader also said 'Heil Hitler' or whether he said 'Guten Morgen' - good morning. My guess is that it was 'Heil Hitler' also. The rooms had to be impeccable. If the leader found one fold on a blanket covering a made bed, he would grab all four bed sheets and pull them down to the floor. He then looked at the open lockers. In the lockers, everything had to be neat; all the clothes on the shelves had to be lined up in a straight line from top to bottom. The shoes and schoolbooks had to be clean and neatly placed at the bottom of the locker. If the clothes were just slightly out of the vertical or one shirt would stick out a little from the rest, all four locker contents would wind up on the floor. We then had until about 7:45 a.m. to put the room back in order for re-inspection, as well as to go down to the dining room for breakfast.

In the whole year, our room only failed one inspection. I guess I was sort of strict, or as strict as an eleven-year-old can be.

The food in the camp was much better than what I would have had at home. All meals were served in the cafeteria, buffet style. We always had to stand in line. However, there was no choice. We all ate the same type of food. There would be only one type of potato if there were potatoes, one type of meat if there was meat, etc. But there was enough food, we could often get seconds if there was food left at the counter. Not only was the food better than in the city, there was also more available. For breakfast we would get porridge, slices of bread with butter and jam, and for drinks, juice and an herb tea. This is perhaps where I developed my love for eating porridge in the morning. At lunchtime we often got 'Eintopf.' This is a German name for a stew-like soup, a thick soup. There was one soup that had cubed chunks of a German blood sausage. That soup was something else. I asked my mother many times, years later, to make this kind of soup but she could never figure out, from my explanations, what the exact ingredients were. So it never worked out for me to taste something as good as was in the camp.

In Germany, and I believe in most European countries, the main meal at that time was, and perhaps still is today for many, the noontime meal. For supper we often had sandwiches. These would be with cheese or cold-cuts. When we had cheese, we often took the cheese off and ate it by itself. We would then put the end of the bread slice between our teeth, and push the butter with our teeth toward the other end of the bread. Sitting on the end would then be a pile of butter, which we ate with the last bite of bread. I think we started this game because when we were at home we never got butter on our bread. The rations were so small at home that the butter was used for cooking and baking. On a few occasions we found in the Swiss-type cheese, the one with the holes in it, little maggots. The maggots were white and about 1/4 inch long. Some kids were a little bit freaked out at that. But the kitchen staff said there was nothing wrong with taking the maggots out of the cheese and eating the cheese, that's what just about everyone did. The ones that wouldn't eat the cheese had no trouble giving their cheese away. The maggots didn't bother me; I just removed the ones I saw.

After breakfast we went to the toilet if we had to and then to the classroom. We had to be in class before 8:00 a.m.; anyone arriving later would have to have a good excuse. Having to remake the room was not considered a good excuse. The classroom was about the right size or even a little bigger than what was needed for forty students. At the front wall of the room, above the blackboard, was a huge pulldown map of Europe. The first hour in the morning was a lecture from the teacher on how well the German troops were doing. Every morning we were told where the troops were advancing. Sometimes the advances were from a location that was fifty kilometres further back than where the Germans had been a week earlier. We were never shown the German troops retreating; it looked like such terminology was not part of the teacher's vocabulary. So, for the rest of the morning we covered reading, writing, arithmetic, history and other subjects. That was school for the day. We did not get all that much homework. Whatever homework we did get was done in the classroom after lunch or supper. At noon we were dismissed to wash up and get ready for lunch. Between noon and 1:00 p.m. we had lunch, did homework and/or took our dirty wash to the laundry, etc. By 1:00 p.m. we had to be in the room on the bed. It was mandatory that we had one hour rest and sleep if possible between 1:00 and 2:00.

At 2:00 p.m. we had to be outside, in front of the building, for our outdoor activities, weather permitting. Our youth leader would be in charge. He would have us stand at attention in line, three rows deep. He would then inform us what he had in mind for the afternoon. Often we marched off away from our camp into the woods. There we often played games, like hide-and-seek. Three or four would take off, get a fifteen-minute head start, and the rest of us would go later to find them. During the summer there was a time, while it was really hot, when we had free time and could go to some small nearby lakes. I was already very comfortable in water. There was only a handful in our class that could swim across the lakes and I was one of them.

I always had this competitive streak in me. I had to try to be as good as or better than others. However, for some reason, this attitude did not include being best in school work when I was a kid. It was more related to physical tasks. I only became fairly ambitious to study and increase my knowledge of things after I left school at age 14. The older I got, the more I felt that trying to outdo everyone at all costs can also be very destructive. Many people don't seem to have that strong urge to beat everyone, even when they have entered a competition; they just want to play along. But, what is strange is that most people defend the right for everyone to become the ultimate winner and that the winner takes all. In our society the winners can take all and become multi-billionaires. Allowing the creation of billionaires perhaps also results in the creation of millions of poor people.

The way the afternoon activities were organized, the four classes very seldom did things together. This was probably because of the age differences between the classes. It seemed to be the responsibility of each youth leader to figure out what he was going to have his group do in the afternoons. After we had become familiar with the territory around the campsite, we were at times allowed to do things on our own in the afternoon. The former resort complex 'Johanneser Kurhaus' where we lived, was located completely isolated, in the high wooded hills of the Harz Mountains. It was located about three kilometres to the west of Clausthal-Zellerfeld, an old lead and zinc mining town with a population of seven or eight thousand. North-west of our camp, about four kilometres away, was Wildemann; a town of less than five thousand. Both small resort towns were mainly involved in providing lodging for people who were vacationing and wanted to hike, who perhaps liked the hilly scenery and fresh clean air. During the winter they were also good ski resorts. The area toward Clausthal had a few abandoned mines, not too far from the road. We were strictly forbidden to enter any of these mines, and no one did as far as I know. There were also lots of slagheaps left over from the mines. On these huge slagheaps were plenty of shiny glistening stones of all colours. In the beginning we thought we had discovered silver or even gold. We would bring back the most impressive pieces to our teacher, only to be told that these were good-looking stones but otherwise worthless. After bringing back better and better specimens, and getting the same answer, we slowly started to not be impressed by the glittering slagheaps any more. One day we also had a trip to Clausthal to enter one of the mines in that town. It had been fixed up as a museum many decades before. There was also a school for miners in the town. We were impressed. To get there we had to walk the three kilometres both ways. It was a well-organized day's outing.

As already mentioned we also had a nurse in the camp. She gave first aid and looked after minor ailments, and was to diagnose whatever else we may have had. I never needed her help. My only contact with her was during showering. All the boys had to take a shower once a week. The shower room was in the basement. It could take about a dozen boys at a time. I don't recall what the time arrangements were, but I remember that I did at times shower with boys from the other classes.

So, over time I saw every one of the 160 boys in the camp naked, at least once. We were all between ten and thirteen years old except maybe two or three boys that had failed a year somewhere and consequently were still in the eighth grade at age fourteen. One of these boys looked different from us, he had lots of hair in his genital area and his penis looked more like our fathers', it was much bigger than ours. In order to shower we had to undress in the basement in a room next to where the shower room was. That room had benches on which we left the clothes, shoes and towels. From there we walked stark naked to the shower room. Well, to our surprise when we took the first shower, we learned that the young good-looking nurse was there to supervise us, to make sure we all showered, and showered properly. She would be standing in the doorway of the shower room. We just about had to pass by her single file, and she seemed to take her job very seriously, at least in the beginning. She would pay very close attention to our activities under the showers. I heard her say once to a boy that he better not forget to wash a certain body part. After two or three weeks, the rumour started that this very-well-endowed boy had been doing some hanky-panky with the nurse. It was not too long after that when we got a new nurse. I never found out whether the rumour was actually true, but I think it was.

Several times in the afternoons when we were free to do whatever we wanted, a few of us would walk down the road to Wildemann. By the way, the literal translation of 'Wildemann' is "wild man." I wonder how they ever got to use that name for this nice little town. The road down to Wildemann was a gravel road, probably used a lot by the lumber industry that was there before the war. There was quite a change in elevation down to this little town, situated in a valley. We would be a handful of friends that went down, roaming the woods next to the road. On the way back from Wildemann I would be playing the gorilla. There were perhaps thirty tall thin trees along one side of the road. They were about forty-five feet tall and fifteen feet apart. I would climb up the first tree to a height of about thirty feet and start swinging the tree back and forth until I got close enough to reach and grab the trunk of the next tree. I did that for about ten trees and then came back down to earth again. There was one other fellow who was doing a little bit of that, but it was mainly I that was doing this to the cheering and shouting of the rest of the boys. I was always a little bit of a daredevil. We had to keep quiet about this activity, because if the camp manager had found out, we, and mainly I, would have been in deep trouble.

During the summer we also spent a lot of time combing the country side, for about a five-kilometre radius. The Allied air forces also conducted a humongous propaganda campaign to convince the German population to quit supporting the Nazis and to rise up against them. In the years 1942, 1943 and 1944 it was perhaps at its peak. The Allied planes dropped leaflets all over Germany. These leaflets were written in German and had a lot of cartoons and pictures on them. They were saying how bad the Nazis were, that Germany would lose the war and that it was hopeless to continue, that Germans should be free from this tyranny and how rosy it would be after the Nazis had been defeated.

Well it was not hard for the Nazis to shoot this type of propaganda down, because of the memory the Germans had from the 1918 capitulation, and how they suffered afterwards, until Hitler got into power. We sometimes were given a lunch bag to take with us and then we spent the whole day combing the countryside to collect these leaflets. We would play little games as to who would find the most leaflets of a certain type, and who would find the most different types. We did not

pay much attention as to what was written on them, the cartoons probably aroused the most curiosity as to what they meant. We would bring
back bags full of these leaflets. The bags were weighed, and the boys
who collected the most would actually get special praise and some sort
of reward. I think it was a piece of cake. This was paper and Germany
had a shortage of just about everything, so these leaflets were collected
to help the German war effort. The day after each collection day it
would be explained to us in class what out and out lies were told on the
sheets and that just the opposite was true.

In addition to collecting leaflets, we also collected aluminium strips
that were dropped by the tons over Germany to make the German
radar ineffective. These aluminium strips were like the 'Lametta,' the
angel-hair on Christmas trees. We collected these strips at the same
time as the leaflets, and actually in much greater quantity. The country
side was just covered with them. The strips did not evoke the same kind
of interest. Of course, collecting this aluminium was also part of the
war effort.

We also had all kinds of games that we played in the open in the
afternoons during the summer. These games were like the hide-and-
seek type, finding-the-enemy games. We also had sport activities,
like running, high-jumping, long-jumping, throwing and climbing
over obstacles. There seemed to be times when our camp leader got
instructions from outside as to what activities we should be involved
in. Or, perhaps the four teachers themselves, perhaps together with the
youth leaders, had some brainstorming sessions to come up with new
activities to make things more interesting for us. There were a couple
of weeks, in the middle of the summer, when we would have some
sort of a competition to come up with songs that could be sung while
marching. These songs were to glorify our fathers' soldiers' actions at

the front. This was in 1943 when it was not yet totally obvious for some people that Germany would lose the war. I came up with some sort of a Panzer (tank) song that would be sung to an existing, popular marching melody. I don't remember getting much praise for it, but of the few songs that were used by our leaders while we were marching, mine lasted the longest, that is, it lasted a few weeks. I forgot the words, but they were somewhat a reworded version of the German song that came out when Field Marshal Rommel's tanks were rolling forward in Africa. My version was more general. By the summer of 1943, the Germans, unable to keep the supply lines, had already retreated from Africa.

In the late summer we had the most enjoyable couple of weeks of the year. One day we were told that we had to go to Wildemann and fix up some rooms in individual houses so that some schoolgirls out of Hannover could be put in them as part of the 'Kinderlandverschickung', the German children evacuation program, to get them away from the bombing. So a couple of days later we were taken by truck down to this little town. It looked like one of these towns that are pictured in fairy tales. The houses were mainly small guest houses in which, during peacetime, the owners would put up tourists all year around. During the summer the tourist came to hike in the hills and during the winter they came to ski. We were divided up into groups of four; actually the boys that were roommates would be together as a group. I guess they figured, this way we knew each other best and should be able to get along best. Each group was then assigned to a house.

We were introduced to the owners of one house, an elderly couple. They showed us their house and the room we had to fix up. They must have been getting something for this, because they also fed us at lunch time, even though food at the time was scarce. Our youth leader was with us for the first half hour to tell us what we had to. We had to remove all the furniture and articles from the room that was meant to become the girls' room. The owners, a very nice couple, told us where to move things to in the house. We had to take all the pictures off the walls etc. When the room was empty, we had to clean it. This included washing the walls and ceiling. Then we had to paint some of the walls. All this took several days. Every day we went back to our camp before supper. So overall we may have spent four to five hours of work per day in the house. It was actually fun. In the evenings at home we would exchange stories with the other kids of what they had experienced during the day. We had lots of laughs. Kids easily find strange and funny the habits and rules that adults often think are of the utmost of importance.

We did have a schedule and we had to have all the rooms ready by a certain day, when the girls were supposed to arrive. After the room we were responsible for was in top shape we had to move in four steel beds that were delivered by truck. I don't remember what the facilities were for the girls to store their clothes. It could have been dressers. All I remember is that they did not have steel lockers like we had.

When the room was completely ready, we were told to decorate it a little, to welcome the girls. We got some flowers and we made a large "welcome" banner. The next day we had to go to the railway station and pick up our girls. Some boys were not all that comfortable with that. I was always sort of reserved with adults, but with girls in a group I was all right. I was less comfortable when I was totally alone with a girl.

When we arrived at the train station, it was an open platform, and had a small station house. We were early and had to wait. When the train arrived, we saw all the girls come out of the railway cars. As we sized up the girls, we wondered who the ones were that we had to introduce to their new home. They were herded into the small station building while the luggage was taken off the train. There they were sorted into groups and told where they would be staying. We were all anxious to meet our girls. After the girls found out who their roommates were, we were introduced and we helped them find their suitcases. We then had to help them get onto the transporting pickup trucks and take them to their new homes. It was all very exciting.

The girls were surprised by the reception they got. But there were no relationships built by anyone from our camp, at least not that I heard about. After all, we were all only ten-to- fourteen-year-old kids. Our place high in the wooded hills was about four kilometres away from Wildemann; this idyllic little town was sitting in a deep valley. Other than walking, we had no transportation to get down there, and our supervisors would never have let us go to see the girls. We never saw them again. However, this whole operation of creating new homes for these girls was a very well organized project.

While I was safe in the camp near Clausthal-Cellerfeld, Hannover experienced its worst air raid of the war. From what I read, up to this point in time Hannover had already had hundreds of air-raid alarms since the beginning of the war. On October 9th, 1943, between 1:05 and 1:45 at night, 540 planes of the Royal Air Force dropped 1,660 tons of bombs. These were 230,000 incendiary bombs, 28,000 phosphorus bombs and 3,000 heavy explosive bombs. Fleeing people got stuck in melted street asphalt and burned to death; that is how hot parts of the city got. The center of the city as well as its south side was almost totally destroyed. 1,245 people lost their lives and many more were wounded. About 250,000 people became 'Obdachlos', having lost their housing. Only ten days later, Hannover experienced another heavy attack.

This is a picture of the main Hannover railway station. It was totally destroyed during the heaviest air-raid of downtown Hannover in the month of October 1943. The aerial photograph was taken by Margaret Bourke-White (USAAF) at the end of the war by which time the rubble had been cleaned away. Under the open square in front of the railway station was an air-raid bunker built for 2,100 people. During the raids there may have been twice as many people in the bunker, but they all survived.

Hannover was one of the cities in Germany best equipped with bunkers. This helped to keep the death-toll low. The same size and type of air-raid attacks in other cities resulted in ten to twenty times as many casualties. At the camp, we kids were not informed about this or any other great losses that Germany suffered. They did not want kids to have to worry about anything. I only found out about the Hannover attacks the next time my mother came to visit me. She could only stay for perhaps a couple of hours and also did not want me to worry, so she would not tell me the worst or too much about what had happened. Of course, one can now get all the details from the city hall of Hannover.

It must have been a day in November 1943 when we played a game of hide-and-seek at the camp. There was already plenty of snow on the ground. Winters in the 3000-foot Harz Mountains were not like those in Hannover. The Harz had real winters. We were instructed the day before that we had to play a big hide and seek game the next day. In the morning after breakfast, two of the oldest boys were told to go and hide somewhere within a two- to three-kilometre radius. They were on skis. The rest of the 160 boys had to leave about an hour later to find them. We had all day to do it. But we had no skis and the two boys we were looking for were fairly good skiers. We got lunch bags to take with us. It was meant to occupy us all day. We were broken up into small groups of six or eight to scour the area. It was not all that easy; at times we sank into the snow above our knees. We were also given a time when we had to return home. Depending what direction the searching boys went, only a few of them would ever find the two skiers; the rest of us would just be looking until they had to turn back to the camp before evening, without even knowing whether anyone had found the two. We got back to the camp before it got dark and found out that the two boys were found and where they had been hiding. Of course, they had left trails wherever they went with their skis, however they also crossed their own tracks several times to confuse the searchers. The two weren't actually found until late in the afternoon, hiding in a large empty stone house. They had broken the glass in a back door to get in. Of course, the ski tracks leading to the house gave them away. I never heard that they received any scolding or punishment for the break-in.

During the year, my mother came to visit me about three times. She also had to visit my sister, who was only about 17 kilometres, by winding road, away from where I was. My sister and I could not see each other. I guess it would not have been reasonable to start letting one kid go visit; in no time others would want to get the same privileges. My mother could not see just one of us and go home the same day; the train trip was too long for that. She had to stay in our area at least for one night. This was easy at my sister's place. She lived in a small tourist town, like Wildemann. I on the other hand was in the woods, three kilometres away from the closest town. My mother had already been going to see my sister in her home in Altenau for almost two years. She had a certain place to stay when she visited, and she already knew some people in the town.

CHAPTER NINE
Leaving the Camp – Living in the Village of my Birth

When Christmas came around in 1943, my mother thought that I should come with her and we celebrate Christmas together at my sister's place. So when my mother arrived at my place a couple of days before the holidays, she went to the camp manager, who was also my teacher. My mother told me that, when she asked the manager if she could take me for two or three days to celebrate Christmas with my sister, he got rude and told her that no child was going to leave his camp. My mother was very annoyed and upset. She had no choice; she had to leave me and go to my sister's place.

However, as soon as she got back home to Hannover she went to the farm village where I was born. She spoke to one of the largest farmers there. These were old friends of my parents; the farmer's wife was even my sister's godmother. My mother went there often during the war when they needed help at planting and harvest time. When she told them how she had been treated by my camp manager, they offered to let me stay on the farm if she were able to get me out of the camp. My mother then went to see the mayor of the farm village and asked him if he could write a letter for the camp leader and request my release, which he did. In the second the week of January,

1944, my mother came back to my camp and handed the letter over to the camp manager. He told her that she was lucky the place she wanted me released to was far enough away from a large city, otherwise he could refuse to let me go. I then packed my belongings, said goodbye to all my friends, and left the camp with my mother on the same day. We took the train and I'm not sure whether we arrived at the farm that same day, but it was the next day for sure. When we arrived, I was given a room all to myself. Of course, whenever my mother came there she would sleep in the same room with me.

This was the beginning of a completely different lifestyle than what I was used to in the camp. I had come back to my place of birth, Schwüblingsen. Although I was born here, I didn't know anybody in this little farm village. I had left the place as a baby about ten years earlier. On the other hand, a lot of people knew about me because of my father; he was known everywhere. The farm family I lived with consisted of the grandmother, who was the mother of the farmer, the farmer, his wife and their two sons. The farmer's first name was Adolf, but although it was the same as 'Adolf,' Germany's 'Führer,' the farmer was a fairly gentle man. It was his wife, Herta, who was more-or-less in charge. I addressed them, as I was told, as 'Tante Herta' and 'Onkel Adolf', aunt and uncle, although we were not related. The older son, also named Adolf, after his father, was about eight years old and his brother, Hans-Jürgen, was five years old.

Adolf, the father, was not in the army because he had a heart condition. He was not able to do any physical work, but he would direct most of the work. His mother was perhaps around eighty. She would do a little bit of garden work but also had a lot to say about the less important items around the house. Every once in a while, when she was in the garden working around the vegetables, she would walk over to a bare patch of ground or onto a grassy area and just stand there with her legs apart. About five seconds later one could see liquid dropping onto the ground between her legs. She was always dressed completely in black; her dress was long enough so that only her ankles showed. When I first saw this performance, I wasn't exactly sure what had gone on. As soon as she left, and I was sure she could not see me, I went over to the spot where she had stood and checked it out. I realized right away that she had relieved herself, and I guessed that she wore no underwear. I later hinted at this to Adolf, the older son, and he confirmed that she always did that whenever she needed, when she worked in the garden. He thought this was quite normal. Weeks later, when I mentioned it to some of the friends I had made by then, we got a good laugh out of it.

The pictures below show Otto's home on the farm in 1944.

This picture was taken on a1960 trip to Germany

This picture was taken in 2006 - Trip to Germany Picture shows
Adolf, he was eight in 1944, and my wife Gertrud

Schwüblingsen was a farm village of perhaps fewer than 500
people. At this point in time, it pretty well consisted only of old
men, women, children and foreigners. The foreigners were from
just about all the countries that had been invaded by Germany
during the Second World War. On our farm there was a big strong
Ukrainian brought to Germany from some area in Ukraine. There
was a Belgian, who was a prisoner of war; he always had to wear his
Belgian uniform, I guess so that he could easily be identified as a
prisoner of war. There was a young Polish woman in her late twenties. And last but not least, a Polish mother with two daughters. One
daughter was about fourteen and the other was perhaps sixteen. All
these people were living on the farm. As I mentioned before,

this was a relatively large farm, even by German standards. The Polish women and the Ukrainian could talk to each other more or less in their own languages, because they are somewhat similar. However, all their communication with the Belgian was in German.

In peacetime, this farmer had to have farm workers living on the farm. Therefore, the rooms that had been used by regular farm workers before the war were now available for these foreign workers. The rooms were off the Diele, a big hall that would be large enough to hold a dance party in. There were four doors off the Diele to the farm helpers' rooms, as well as doors to the cow stables, the horse stable, the laundry room/pigsty and the main house's hallway. The Diele was large and tall enough to accommodate a fully loaded hay wagon with room to spare. Actually, the hay wagons would be brought into the Diele to store hay above the cow and horse stables, as well as above the Diele itself and the rooms attached to it. This Diele could be compared to the main hall in a castle where festivities could be held. The ceiling was high and had large wooden beams across it. In the upper corners of the beams which were close to the huge entrance door, swallows would build their nests. There were at any one time about a dozen nests up there, not all of them occupied.

Although the large entrance door was normally closed, the peoples' door within the large door would normally be open. So the swallows would dive in and out of the Diele through that relatively small peoples' door. There were always chirping noises in the Diele, but one didn't pay attention to them after a while, they were just part of the Diele. If the chirping would have stopped, one would have wondered if there was something wrong. It was easy to know which nests were currently occupied; one only had to look down to the floor to see the bird droppings and then glance up to the see the nest above.

These swallows were fascinating to watch. They would dive out through the entrance, soar up above the courtyard, catch an insect and bring it back to feed their young. Both, male and female partners would be doing this. They were good weather forecasters, not for the next day but for the next few hours. Depending on the air pressure, the insects would be high up in the air during good weather, but as a low-pressure air mass approached the insects would fly lower and lower and so did the swallows in order to catch them.

The Diele always had that stale, musky kind of smell; it was not objectionable to farm-grown people, I guess they didn't even notice it. It was not all that bright in the Diele either. The only daylight coming in was through the people-entrance, and during the evening a single bare bulb hanging from the ceiling prevented it from being completely dark. The walls and ceiling probably had had their last lime-whitewash application twenty years earlier. The rooms for the help were not fancy, but they had what one would need to exist. There were beds, closets, dressers, tables and chairs in them. These rooms were right and left off the Diele in the front part of the main house. In order to get to the farmer's portion of the house, where I also lived, one had to go through the Diele. The door at the end then led to a corridor in the farmer's living portions of the house. This door could be locked, and I guess at night it was locked.

All the foreigners worked six days a week except for the two Polish girls. But the older sixteen year old would pitch in quite a bit too. I'm not sure whether by the Nazi rules she was required to work. The Ukrainian almost acted as if the farm was his, he was very reliable. He more or less knew what had to be done and how best to do it. He would discuss the work with Adolf at times but always with Herta's important input and final word.

Tante Herta was a big woman; she had this strange kind of walk. It was sort of wobbling from side to side like a duck. I guess she was shifting her weight from one leg to the other, with her legs somewhat apart. In the back of the big farmhouse was a big garden. This had fruit trees as well as a large vegetable plot. One of the things I remember about this garden was that in one corner was a brick-walled pit – 5 feet high, 15 feet wide and 20 feet long, with one side open. The bottom of the pit was about a foot below ground level. The pit was filled with alternate layers of Mangelwurzels or mangold wurzel and their leaves. Their large white, yellow or orange-yellow swollen roots were developed in the 18th century as a fodder crop for feeding livestock. Mangelwurzel is mainly used to feed cattle in Europe. This layered arrangement was put into the pits when the beets were harvested. The whole thing was left alone until the winter when small portions, one or two wheel-barrows full, were taken out every day to become part of the feed for the cows. It lasted all winter, which was the time the cows were in the stables instead of in the pastures. This stuff, when it was in the pit for months, started to smell very sour, especially after they had started removing portions of it. One could easily smell the pit from at least fifty feet away. The beets did not rot for some reason; I am not sure whether there was something spread onto the layers to prevent any rotting. But the sour smell was strong and not the type of smell next to which one would be able to eat a sandwich. But the cows loved it.

The Ukrainian was also the 'Schweizer' or 'Melker', the milker who milked the cows. There were more than forty-five cows, fifty pigs, five horses, twenty rabbits, some ducks, geese and I don't know how many chicken on this farm. So food was no problem. The Ukrainian, and pretty well all the adults, would get up around six o'clock. By the time I got up around seven, all except the two boys had had their breakfast already. The Ukrainian by that time was already on his way to the pastures to milk the cows. The pastures were about two kilometres away from the village. There was a small milk wagon that was specially designed to be pulled by the farm's watchdogs. These were two large German shepherd dogs. They normally were tied to long chains that would reach almost across the entrance passage to the huge farmhouse front courtyard. The cobblestoned courtyard was about 200 by 200 feet square and surrounded by the farm buildings. Facing the street was a huge, approximately 120- by 50-foot, hay barn. To the left of that hay barn was the entrance to the yard, with the doghouse on the left side of the entrance. After entering the yard, on the right side was a long, low building with more than ten pigsties. On the left side was a huge building, mainly for storing all their farm equipment. At the opposite side from the entrance, which is on the far side of the yard, was the main house, with the cow stables on the left and the horse stable on the right. It was a well laid-out farmhouse complex, with the huge yard in the middle. Whenever someone not belonging to the farm family or workers, appeared at the entrance the watchdogs, and they were big, would make enough noise so that the person normally would not dare to step onto the property. The barking was audible almost anywhere inside the buildings.

So, the Ukrainian would take these dogs, put a harness on them and hitch them to the milk wagon. He would load about eight large milk cans, able to hold about forty litres each, onto the wagon and then climb on it himself. It was just as if this was a miniature horse-drawn rig. The dogs would pull the wagon the two kilometres to the pastures where the cows were grazing. This was not too bad for the dogs when the dirt road near the pastures was dry and the cans were empty. But during or after a good rain, and with full cans, the wagon often got stuck. The milker would then get off the wagon and help pushing. At that time I didn't think about how tough the dogs' lives were, but today I still feel sorry for them. The saying 'dog's life', implying a life that is considered terrible for humans, really applied to these two dogs. I always liked dogs, and I considered it a pleasure to be able to feed those dogs. They were always tied to their doghouse, except when they were pulling the wagon. They would get fed after the people on the farm had their meals; the dogs got the leftovers, which was really not that bad on this farm.

The cows had to be milked twice each day, once early in the morning and again late in the afternoon. Every once in a while in the afternoon the milker would ask me if I wanted to come along. When I did, I also sat on the wagon, making it even harder for the dogs. But I enjoyed these trips. When we got to the cow pastures, we first had to herd the cows to the section where the milking barn was located. I can't imagine, even now, anyone wanting to suck the milk out of an animal's tits. Yet people find it quite normal to have someone else or, have machines squeeze milk out of animal tits and then drink it. I was quite happy at the time to take a small cup and scoop a few mouthfuls out of the milk buckets.

There were about six huge, fenced off pasture sections. The cows would be rotated from one section to another every few days so that the grass had a chance to recover. Every month the liquid manure from the farm house would be spread onto one or two of the sections that did not have cows on them. Maybe only about twenty-five of all the forty-five cows had to be milked. The milker knew exactly which cows we had to herd in and I wondered how he knew which ones he had to milk. He would call and talk to them by name. Every cow, in the herd of more than forty cows, even the calves, had names, and he knew them all.

This was perhaps one of the ten largest farmers in Schwüblingsen. There were only about 30 farms in the village. Each one had from between four to six foreigners as workers. These were a mixture from just about all of the countries that Germany had occupied during the war. By 1944, foreigners in Germany made up 26.4 percent of the total workforce. Already in 1944, if not even earlier, they knew that Germany was going to lose the war. It is therefore amazing that they did not revolt or at least sabotage things in the village. During the year that I was in the village there were maybe only two independent cases where men had some sort of fights, verbally, with the people they worked for. It would have been easy for anyone to call the police and get armed help quickly.

The State knew exactly where all foreigners were, and all the Germans for that matter. Everyone in Germany was registered. If a foreigner was not at the place where he was supposed to be, the farmer, or in most cases the farmer's wife, because her husband was in the army, was expected to report it immediately to the police. There would be police asking the farmers every once in a while whether everything was in order.

These foreign workers were often working by themselves kilometres away from the village, from sunrise to sunset during the harvest. These workers had their lunches, milk and snacks for breaks with them. On the whole, these foreigners had it perhaps better than the German people in the bigger cities that were constantly being bombed. Also, food-wise they were much better off on these farms than the German city dwellers. Thinking back, this farmer treated these foreign workers just as well as if they had been German workers.

This village was about thirty kilometres from Hannover. As already mentioned, King George Louis of Hannover also became George I, King of England. At that time the German spoken in the kingdom of Hannover was not too far away from the spoken English. The whole of central European Germanic tribes were called Saxons by the Romans. The area then became Sachsen and later the area of the King of Hannover became Niedersachsen or Lower Saxony in English. These people from Sachsen and any member of the Germanic peoples inhabited and ruled England from the 5th century AD to the time of the Norman Conquest (1066). According to the Venerable Bede, the Anglo-Saxons were the descendants of three different Germanic peoples 'the Angles, Saxons, and Jutes' who originally migrated from northern Germany to England in the 5th century at the invitation of the British chieftain Vortigern to defend his country against Pictish and Irish invaders. Their subsequent settlements in what is now England laid the foundation for the later kingdoms of Essex, Sussex, and Wessex (Saxons), East Anglia, Middle Anglia, Mercia, and Northumbria (Angles), and Kent (Jutes). The various Anglo-Saxon kingdoms spoke dialects of what is now known as Old English. Ethnically, the 'Anglo-Saxons' actually represent an admixture of Germanic peoples with England's pre-existing Celtic inhabitants and subsequent Viking and Danish invaders.

The term 'Anglo-Saxon' seems to have been first used by continental writers in the late 8th century, to distinguish the Saxons of Britain from those of the European continent, whom the Venerable Bede had called Antiqui Saxones ('Old Saxons'). After the Norman Conquest, the term simply came to mean 'the English.' The name formed part of a title, rex Angul-Saxonum ('king of the Anglo-Saxons'), which was sometimes used by King Alfred (AD. 899) and was revived by 11th-century kings.

In this area the people of the older generation could speak Plattdeutsch or "Low German," a German that was probably spoken at the time when the king of Hannover also became the king of England. Low German, with no single modern literary standard, was the spoken language of the lowlands of northern Germany. It developed from Old Saxon and the Middle Low German speech of the citizens of the Hanseatic League. The language supplied the Scandinavian languages with many loanwords, but, with the decline of the league, Low German declined as well. Although the numerous Low German dialects are still spoken in some of the homes of northern Germany and a small amount of literature is written in them, no standard Low German literary or administrative language exists.

The farmer's mother, the one without undies, spoke this Plattdeutsch all the time. It took me some time to figure out what she was talking about. But because her son, daughter-in-law and grandchildren always replied in Hochdeutsch - High German - I caught on. It was only when I came to Canada and learned English that I realized how close Low German is to English. She would say door instead of Tür, meaning door in English.

When I got to this village in January 1944, I was looked at by the grownups as 'this city slicker', who was probably going to spoil their innocent village kids. Well, in a way this totally groundless opinion probably stemmed from the reputation my father had. I think it did me some good. They were the not so timid boys and girls that I made friends with right away. I guess they thought they could learn something from me, me coming from the big city, Hannover. Of course I enjoyed the attention I got. To impress the girls, I always tried to look my best. To make my hair look neat, I started to make up a little sugar water solution and sprinkled a little of that on my hair every morning. It gave me the neatly-combed-hair look all day. Actually I started the sugar water treatment because I wanted to have a little wave in my hair on the right side of the head. After making my hair wet with the sugar water, I pushed the hair forward with my right hand, holding the front with my left hand to create the first wave. Then I put my left-hand index finger into the first fold and repeated the pushing forward with my right hand to create the second wave. The hair stayed that way because it was wet and as it was drying the sugar glued it together. It didn't matter how much the wind blew, my hair always looked combed. It was stiff. I did this for about a year, the time I was in Schwüblingsen. Nobody ever commented on it at the time. However, my sister made some fun about it after the war. Nevertheless, these waves stayed in my hair, without sugar-water, for at least another fifteen years. I have the pictures to prove it.

I also met, for the first time since I was a tiny baby, the girl of the millionaire father with whom my father had that pact to switch us. The arrangement was that, if that girl had been a boy and I had been a girl, we were supposed to be switched. My parents completely lost contact with these people over the ten or so years since we moved to Hannover. I now found out, that which my mother knew but never mentioned – that the girl had Down's syndrome. Germans at the time called it the 'Englische Krankheit,' literally translated the 'English sickness.' Yet, when I looked up the words 'Englische

Krankheit' now in a couple of German dictionaries it translated into English as rickets. Kids that had Down's syndrome at that time were often called mongoloids in English.

This girl, the same age as I was, twelve years old at the time, was as tall as an eight-year-old and she was retarded. She never went, actually couldn't go, to school. How differently life is dished out at times. It was said that the girl's father had become an alcoholic and had squandered away the millions they had. The two brothers of the girl were about sixteen and seemed to belong with the tougher, mischievous kids in the village. When I saw the girl for the first time she was in a baby carriage that one of her older brothers was pushing. I felt so sorry for her. The family lived in a very small farmhouse but had no farm land. They had two ponies and a small carriage that the ponies pulled around the village once in a blue moon.

There were about forty to fifty kids of school age, in this small village, from ages six to fourteen. All eight class levels sat in one class room. I believe the eighth class consisted of five students; a couple were at the age of fourteen, who had to repeat a year. In the seventh class, the one I was in, we were seven students, four girls and three boys. The classroom had about eight rows of benches, broken by an aisle in the middle.

The benches had tables in front to write on, and as I remember, the table tops could be lifted up so one could put books into the wells underneath. Each seat had its own separate table. There was a solid four inch wide strip in front, which had an inkwell in it. Each bench had four seats and we all were assigned a specific seat. Looking from the front of the class room, the boys were seated on the left side of the aisle and the girls on the right. When it came time to sit on the bench, one had to enter from the aisle, and we had to allow those closest to the wall to get in first. If anyone had to go to the washroom, the ones sitting closer to the aisle had to get out first to let them exit.

The eighth-class benches were in the back of the room and the first-class benches were in the front. So when the teacher was in front of the students, he would be closest to the little ones, the six year olds, and farthest away from the oldest in the back of the room.

It was perhaps a little trickier for the teacher to keep order in a class like that. Looking back, I'm still amazed how well it went. When he was verbally teaching one class, the other classes had to have some work to do to keep busy. The last two sets of benches had the larger kids. I, being in the seventh class, was sitting in the second row from the back. These two rows did just about everything together. I remember that the subjects the seventh and eighth grades were taught were often the same. We, the twelve and thirteen year olds, also played together in the schoolyard during the breaks and away from school. In school, during our breaks – I believe we had two a day – we played a game with a medicine ball. In the schoolyard we would set up two fields of equal size, about twenty by twenty feet in area. The girls would stand in one field and the boys in the other. One or two players would also be on the outside ends. One side would then throw this fifteen-pound medicine ball at a person in the opposing field. If the receiving person was hit and could not hold on to the ball but let it drop to the ground that person then had to leave the field and go to the opposite end. The ball was thrown back and forth like that until one side had no more players in its field. This team was then the loser. This looks like an unfair game, the boys playing against the girls. However, no one who played or watched us play, like the teacher, saw anything wrong, we were quite even. The girls were on average older and bigger.

We also had to play sports in school. It was considered important to be healthy, and therefore everyone in school had to participate. I was relatively small for my age but I was good in throwing, I could throw a tennis ball more than 80 metres, 265 feet. That was considered far for a 12 year old. I could climb, throw the heavy medicine ball and swim well, but I was not too good in running, or high- and long-jumping. One day we were going to have a major event, but only the kids from our village participated. We talked and tried to prepare for this event. One of the events was a three-kilometre long distance run. I was always good in endurance types of events; I seemed to get stronger as time went on during an event. To prepare for the long distance run, everyone, including the teacher, said that one has to conserve energy at the beginning and leave plenty in reserve for the sprint at the end. Well I was not a good sprinter. I wasn't tall enough.

So when we were running on this track around the sports field, I just thought that the pace we were going at was much too slow. We had done about one of the six or so laps when it just came to me that I could average a much faster pace. As I increased my pace and separated from the group, we were only six or seven boys, I could hear them mumble that I would not get very far at that pace and they would catch up with me soon. At my pace, which felt comfortable to me, after the field had run another lap, I was a half of a lap ahead of them. I kept that distance out in front for the rest of the race. Everyone then thought that I knew more about long distance racing and that I had kept that knowledge for myself. I felt quite good about the race, but I think if they had not been warned to take it easy at the beginning, they probably would have gone with me at my pace and then beat me at the end. This was the only long distance race we ran during that summer and that was perhaps a good thing for me; they would not have let me go like that a second time.

From the spring of 1944 on our male teacher got a helper. She was a young nineteen-year-old lady who wanted to become a teacher. Or, maybe she preferred teaching instead of army duty. I hit it off well with her right away; she somehow liked me and I thought that I got some special attention from her. Maybe it was because I was different from the others, I did not live with my parents, and because of that maybe she felt sorry for me. Also perhaps it was all in my imagination. But the school girls who were my age also liked me. One day instead of having school the older four classes went on a field trip. It was the lady teacher who took us on this all-day trip. We went over meadows and small bushy areas. When it came time to have lunch, we stopped in an area that had small trees and large bushes. The kids could do whatever they wanted, eat their lunch if they had any left by then, or play etc. The teacher took me aside and asked me to sit down with her on the blanket she brought. We were next to a bush more or less isolated from the others. She then gave me some of her bread, although I had my own. She seemed to be flirting with me, or at least that's what I was imagining. She was asking me all kinds of questions about myself. I was too reserved with adults and did not respond as I would have maybe if I had been a few years older. She knew that I was by myself in this village, maybe she felt sorry for me. I hope not. Years later I always thought maybe I should have exploited this situation, but then again years later when I wound up in similar situations I still could not bring myself to exploit them either. I'm just not my father's son in this department.

The kids in those days did many stupid things which they thought were exiting because they were forbidden. However, today children are sometimes involved in worse things, even in real crimes, which did not seem to be the case then. The adults were a lot stricter with kids then and maybe that has something to do with it. Our pranks were not intended to hurt anyone. At that time just about every household had a carbide lamp, especially during the war when power could be lost at any time through the bombing. So this calcium carbide, used as fuel for the lamps, was available everywhere. The carbide looked like little white and grey gravel stones. A few of those stones would be put into a lamp, water would be added and the mixture produced acetylene gas. The lamp had a valve to control the amount of gas released. These lamps had sort of a metal gauze through which the acetylene escaped. When lit the gauze would almost turn white. It made a perfect lamp.

Well, we made it a point to collect small medicine bottles that had necks just big enough so that one could barely push in green, unripe cherries. We would put two or three carbide stones into such a medicine bottle, add about a teaspoonful of water, and then quickly push in a green cherry into the neck of the bottle. When the pressure built up high enough the cherry would shoot out with a thump and fly perhaps a hundred feet or more. We would aim at each other or at some target. As soon as the cherry came out we would put another one in and shoot until there was no more gas created in the bottle. All we had to do was put in new stones and add water to keep on shooting. So we would have a small container with calcium carbide stones in one pocket, and a container with water in another pocket plus one bag or pocket full of cherries. During one of these foolish games, one of the younger boys was playing around with a bottle and had a bad accident. He must have pushed in a cherry that was too tight. When enough pressure built up the bottle exploded. A large glass splinter went into the hand he was holding the bottle in and another one went into his eye. The hand was badly damaged and he lost his eye. That stirred up the grownups quite a bit. The fact that we had been stealing the green cherries from the farmers' cherry trees did not help either. For a while we were watched by everyone in the village. By the time things had settled down a bit the cherries were too large and too soft for our game.

We also got into a potato throwing game once in a while. We would take a straight stick or tree branch about three feet long and make one end pointy. After sticking a potato onto the pointy end of the stick the potato could be hurled quite a distance, perhaps 50 percent further than throwing the potato by the bare hand. Throwing was always my forté. With the stick I could probably hurl the potato close to 400 feet. Often some of these potatoes would land on a terracotta-shingled roof, and once in a while break a shingle. At times we picked a high barn roof and competed to see who could throw best over that roof. There were always potatoes around in this farm village. But that does not mean that the farmers had to be enthusiastic about our game, especially when these were their potatoes, and windows or shingles that got broken.

A bunch of the older teenagers played a bad prank on one of the farmers. All the boys in this village between fourteen and eighteen had to be working in some sort of apprentice-ship. It was these boys who did this prank, and the two brothers of the former million-aire were supposed to have been the ring leaders. For the May 1 celebration, they took a farmer's hay wagon completely apart and, in the dark, reassembled it straddling the ridge of the farmer's high hay barn roof. The sight of this was unbelievable. On the apex of this barn, nearly thirty feet above the ground, stood this hay wagon. Because of the war, there were no able, healthy German men in this village to get this wagon down; however, it was dismantled somehow.

This was a year in my life that seemed more eventful than the ones before, or maybe I was at the age where the events stuck in my head more than before. By this time in my life, age twelve, I was already keen about going swimming wherever I had the opportunity. Just at the outskirts of the village there was a pond. It was actually a pond that was two thirds surrounded by swamp. It was also in a large cow pasture, and the cows in this pasture like to go into the pond to cool off at times. In the summer, when it was really hot, we would go there and take a dip in the water. It wasn't all that deep, but it cooled us off a little. The bottom was a morass so that one would sink in about six inches of mud, and the water looked brown; it was swampy. And the pond stank a little, almost like manure. But it cooled us off. Every time I got home from this pool, I had to wash myself to get the smell off. I would take a hose and shower myself. When I looked at this pond about twenty years later I was amazed. How, I thought to myself, could anyone swim in that mud bath?

We also had another place to go swimming, Ölerse, on the river Fuhse. To get there we would have to walk more than five kilometres. We didn't fallow the road. We went right across fields and pastures. That way, not following the paved road, we saved at least a kilometre of walking. This was a trip that only the boys participated in; we were always four or five. It was during summer school break and when we had nothing else to do on some days. That is, during the war, the school kids often had plenty of work assigned, helping with the farm work or the war effort. I will describe that later. The one thing I was really glad about was that in this village we did not have any 'Jungvolk' duty, like I had in Hannover in 1942. There were not enough kids around for the Jungvolk, or Hitlerjugend, to come together as an organized group.

Ölerse was a much larger place than the farm village we lived in. It was a small town, yet it also had farmers. But we didn't have to go to the town. Far enough away from the town was a little dam and a water mill. From the part of the river where we were we couldn't even see any of the houses of the town. I guess that was because Ölerse was above the dam where we swam. Where we first got to the river was at least 500 feet from the mill, on the downstream side of the dam. At that point, the river was about a hundred feet wide. On the other side of the river were a few tall trees. One of them had a large branch that reached way out over the water, at a height of at least fifteen feet. We would leave our clothes on our side of the river and then swim across to get to the tree with the overhanging branch. Not everyone would climb up on this tree and jump into the water, but I had to. Whenever there was a challenge I had to try it. The thing I lost during these swims was the sugar in my hair, but that was fixed as soon as I came home. But, one may believe it or not, those two waves that I pressed into my hair with the sugar water stayed with me pretty well for several years, I still have a little bit today.

We were pretty happy with this activity for a few times when we went there. Then one day someone got the idea that we should swim toward the mill, which we did. On the downside of the mill and dam was a pond about two or three times as wide than the river.

At the point where the water came over the dam and also out of the mill, the current was much stronger. It was fun to swim against this current and see who could get to the upstream side first. So we really enjoyed swimming in this pond also. The water was so clean, or at least it looked so clean, that we even drank from it.

However, when we got to the pond the last time, we weren't there long when some older boy yelled at us to take off. We slowly moved back to where our clothes were. By the time we got dressed there were three of these boys yelling at us to take off and never to return, this was their place. They knew where we came from, and we had encroached on their territory. Were these dogs marking their territory? It is amazing how possessive people can be and how this is already instilled in their kids.

We westerners expect to travel all over the world in underdeveloped countries and expect to trot around just about anywhere without anyone's objection. However, we cannot do that in any of our own so-called civilized, industrialized countries, we have demarcation lines everywhere. What problem did we present to those older kids? What does that tell us about ourselves?

Because these boys were a little older, they were therefore bigger than us. We were about two more in number but they were bigger. When they started to throw stones at us, we threw stones back at them. Because they were bigger, they could throw a little further. However, I was perhaps the best and farthest thrower on our side. For that reason I got perhaps more attention from the other side. We would wind up in two opposing lines about 200 feet apart, just far enough to see the stones coming so that we could duck. While throwing stones at each other, these boys from Ölerse drove us all the way back to just the outside of our village. It was a stone throwing battle that went 4 kilometres over fields and pastures, lasting about two hours. Nobody got hurt and we did not say anything to the adults when we got home. But we told some of the older, sixteen-year-old, boys and coaxed a couple of them to come with us the next day. Well, the next day the opposing side was again ready for us. They also had a few even older boys, so, we lost again. That was the end of going swimming in the Fuhse at Ölerse.

In 1944, because the able German men were all at the fronts, the children in the farm villages in Germany had to pitch in during the planting and harvesting time. The ten-year- old and older kids would be transported to some farmers' fields during the planting of potatoes and other crops in the spring. We were told a week in advance that, for the following week, instead of school we would have to go into fields and plant crops. The kids didn't mind. I thought it was more fun than sitting in the classroom. We would take our lunches with us and often we got even better lunches than if we were going to school. Even when it was raining a little at times we had a lot of fun. We would be singing songs at times and doing a lot of making jokes of each other. There were also a lot of grownups with us, even foreign workers, because there were only perhaps 25 kids in school that were old enough for this field work. The fields were huge. In addition to the farm work, we also had to go across the fields and through the woods and gather the leaflets and the radar jamming aluminium strips that were dropped by the American and British planes, just like we had to do in the Harz Mountains. There was a time when we had to pick potato larvae from the potato fields. These larvae were attached to the potato plant leaves and if left there would hatch and destroy the plant, and there would be no potato crop. The potato beetles were not native to Europe; they were native to North America. They did not exist in Germany until the later years of the war. We were told that they were dropped by American planes, to destroy Germany's potato crops. I have never been able to find publications that would corroborate this. It was always denied by the Americans.

All this work was done instead of going to school. Of course, when we did go back to school the leaflets were explained to us, how they contained only propaganda and lies. During the summer, we had time off from school, summer break, and did all kinds of crazy things. The farmers in Germany were dictated to as to what crops and how much of each crop they had to plant during the war. Consequently, they also planted tobacco and poppies. Planting the poppy was to get oil from the poppy-seeds. Germany does not have a warm enough climate to grow any of the warmer climate crops, and it was blockaded to prevent importing anything from outside its borders and from outside of the occupied lands' borders. So the Germans had to be inventive and produce many things the hard way, which will be mentioned later. It would be unthinkable to do this today when things can be imported at a minute fraction of the cost. In 1944 some of the German tanks were running on charcoal, because Germany was running short of diesel oil. These charcoal burners were large contraptions mounted on the back of the tanks. I can't imagine what a problem it must have been to organize the supply of charcoal for refuelling these tanks.

In January of 1944 my sister turned fourteen, which meant that she had to graduate from primary school at the end of March. That also meant that she was not allowed to stay in the Kinderlandverschickung, the child-evacuation-program. Consequently, she was sent back to Hannover to have her confirmation and then to go and do her one year Pflichtjahr, a compulsory service year in some sort of domestic job. There was no choice; all girls had to go through this during the Nazi era. I now think this was an excellent way to teach girls, at the early age of fourteen, to become very familiar with housework and how to work together with people. Often they learned how to look after young kids and babies. One positive thing the Nazis did was keep kids and teenagers occupied in a very beneficial way for the kids; they learned to take on some responsibility. During the week when my sister was tested in order to be confirmed, my father was at home in Hannover on a short leave from the front, for the first time in three years.

I was on the farm that year, but somehow I was also in Hannover for a few days at this time, although I don't remember for what reason. My sister told me that my father took her to the church community house where the girls were tested, to see whether they had enough knowledge of the Christian Religion to be confirmed. She told me that my father got all dressed up for this occasion. He wore a suit and a black top hat. My father was from a sort of 'the twenties type of school', at least in the way he dressed in black with a top-hat. When they arrived at the community house and waited in the lobby I guess, my sister heard one of the girls say to her mother 'ma, is that man a chimney sweep?' We still get a kick out of that when we talk about our father.

It was also at this time that my father was home in March 1944 for a few days. My parents went to see a movie in a theatre just a block away from where we lived. It was in the evening and I was not allowed to see the film. The next morning my parents talked a lot about the 'Wochenschau,' the newsreel, they saw in the theatre. The Wochenschau was always shown in theatres before the main film. It was the only way one could see moving news pictures of what went on in the world. Often by the time one saw the newsreels the event could have already been weeks old. Today, on TV, young people can watch almost instantly what takes place anywhere around the world; wherever cameras can be taken. The Wochenschau (the German week's news show) was used by the Nazis as one of their propaganda media as well. They always showed what looked good for Germany and bad for the Allies. If the Germans were on the losing end of a battle, they would show the brutality of the enemy. Is it any different today?

My parents thought that they had seen a glimpse of a young soldier who looked like one of my father's relatives who had been killed on the Russian Front shortly before. The next day, my father went to the theatre and asked if we could see the newsreel, and perhaps get one negative of the man. The projectionist was very obliging and mentioned he could cut a couple of frames out and we could keep them and perhaps have prints made from them. That afternoon my parents and I went to the theatre and right into the projection booth to watch the newsreel. We were looking through the little windows in the projection booth at the main screen. When the film got to the section where my parents thought they saw the soldier the projectionist slowed the film down and eventually stopped at the frames in which they thought they recognised the soldier. Having the film stopped and looking at it frame by frame, my parents changed their minds and came to the conclusion that it was not the relative whom they thought it was. I did not know the fellow so I had no idea who they were talking about. My saddened parents and I left the theatre.

154

My sister was confirmed in the Markuskirche, the same church in which I was going to be confirmed two years later. However, my father could not be present for my sister because shortly after the test he had to leave again for the front. Now my mother had to contact the Arbeitsamt, the employment office, and find a place where my sister could do her Pflichtjahr, her one year compulsory service. Because of the bombing, she was not allowed to stay in Hannover. So my mother found a farmer in Schwüblingsen, where I was, who needed domestic help. This was also one of the larger farmers in the village; it was Elfi's parents' farm, a girl in my class at school.

However, every time my mother came to visit us my sister was crying her eyes out. The farmer's wife was very mean to her. Within six weeks of when she started the job, my mother went back to the employment office, to find an alternate place for her to do her one year compulsory service. Because my sister had three years' experience living in a camp type of organization, she was sent to a camp in Hohegeiss, again in the Harz Mountains. This was a small town about 150 km southeast of Hannover, even further away than Altenau, the place where she was before. When she got there, they had her work in the kitchen at first. However, they then considered her three year camp experience, and decided to have her look after the kids in the camp. She stayed in this camp until the one year of compulsory domestic service was up, which was in March 1945.

Any one of these family get-togethers could easily have been the last one. Of the 5.5 million German soldiers who fought on the eastern front, fewer than one million returned home. Ten years after the war, in 1955, of the 1,250,000 soldiers missing on the Russian front, 1,000,000 were written off as dead. Of the German soldiers captured by the Russians and sent to Siberia, 90 percent did not return. I personally heard only of friends' and neighbours' fathers and sons that did not come back from the Russian front. I never heard of one soldier that had survived the Russian prisoner of war camps and came home.

Coming back to my life in Schwüblingsen, as already mentioned, we did smoke the odd cigarette, when we could get ahold of one. So, in the summer, when the tobacco leaves were large and nearly ready to be harvested, we, my friends and I, went to pick a handful each to dry them somewhere. We had to make sure the grownups would not see us with these leaves. So we went into the woods about half a kilometre outside of the village and dug a five-by-five-foot hole into the ground. It was about four feet deep and had dirt benches on the sides. We put some logs over the top and covered the whole thing with boards, branches, soil and leaves. This was going to be our hideaway. It had a small entrance that was easy to close and hide. One had to really be wondering what this little raised ground area was, before becoming suspicious and discovering this hideout. Well, we thought this was a perfect place to dry our tobacco leaves, and later smoke them. We carefully spread the leaves out on the dirt benches. Somehow we didn't get back to this place for some time.

However, when we did go back three weeks later we found the leaves had started to rot, they were limp, had changed colour and actually were much damper then when we left them there. We realized this was not a place to dry anything and we abandoned it. But, we didn't have that much trouble getting tobacco or cigarettes anyway. We found the places where the grownups were drying their leaves, and Horst, one of my best friends, had parents who had a sort of a grocery store, in which they were selling cigarettes as well. This was a similar situation I had in Hannover where, Walter, also one of my friends, had parents who had a tobacco store. The friend in this village also had a sister who was a year older. She had failed one year and consequently was in my class and sitting on the same bench-row in school, except on the other side of the aisle.

We were a group of three boys and four girls who hung out together. If I remember the names right, it was Heinrich, Horst and I, Horst's sister Waltraut, Elfi – short for Elfriede – Inge and another Waltraut. Elfi was not as good looking as the other girls; however I did have a short affair with her after the war, about four years later. We would meet occasionally after supper in the evenings during spring and fall when school was on, and frequently in the middle of the day during the summer break. But on weekends we almost always met and strolled around together through the woods. A lot of times we kidded each other. We had a lot of fun.

When just a boy and girl happened to be alone, it would, at least for me, become a little awkward, I was a little bit on the shy side when alone with a girl. Occasionally there was a little kiss stolen, but really in a most innocent way. After all, we were only twelve and thirteen. At times this was done in a haystack in one of the barns. Most of the time when we were together we would be three boys, but often one or two of the girls couldn't make it. The two youngest girls, my age, lived just a bit outside the village. They were the tallest of the group. They were not related but they looked and acted like sisters. I liked them the most, although they were about five inches taller than I was. The brother and sister, Horst and Waltraut, were able to get ahold of some cigarettes every once in a while, their parents had that grocery store. We would then go away from the village and smoke them.

In the fall when the poppy was getting ripe, we would sneak into the fields that were close to the village and stuff ourselves full with poppy seeds. We would eat them by the handful until we were full. It is from the sap of the poppy heads that opium is made in some countries. Germans grew and harvested the poppy seeds for the oil that was pressed out of them. Well, when we stuffed ourselves with the seeds, we would get sick for a couple of days. We got diarrhoea. However, we could not tell anyone that we had been in the field stealing poppy seeds. With respect to how we got the diarrhoea, we just played ignorance. When we felt normal again after a few days, we would go back and again stuff ourselves, until all the poppies had been harvested, which lasted for about two weeks.

We, boys and girls, also went into the forest, which was about two kilometres away from the village. In the late summer the forest was full of blueberries. We would go there with buckets and bring them back home full of berries. These blueberries seemed to be much larger than what one would find in stores. They were actually easy to pick, all one had to do was let the little branches slip through the fingers and the berries would be left in the hand. We had lots of fun picking and horsing around together. These berries were free, the woods belonged to the county, and no one ever got stopped picking them. Even my mother would come from Hannover to pick these blueberries when they were ripe. In the forest there were also downed bombers, about three, spread over an area of about ten square kilometres. I guess they were left there because they were not that easy to get out of the woods. Any plane that crashed in a farmer's field would have been removed fairly quickly. We were told not to even go close to these crashed planes, but we couldn't help it, the curiosity was too great. These planes were more or less burned out and pretty well broken up over large areas. There was never anything at these sites that was useful to us. Sometimes we would pick up a small piece of metal that had a special shape or colour.

In the fall when school started up again we had to study history. The two upper grade levels, seven and eight, studied many of the same subjects together. I did not like school that much before, but being together with the girls in the same class seemed to spurn me on a little more than when I was only with boys the years before. I wanted the girls to think that I was not a dummy. The farmer where I lived had an old history book that I could borrow. The history we studied was from the crusades to about the 19th century. In terms of schoolwork, I had no support from the people where I lived, I was on my own. Whenever my mother would visit, she would look at my schoolwork, but I don't recall me having any real problems with any subject anymore. I started to enjoy history then and still enjoy it today. The history book was as large and thick as a bible and had many pictures in the form of copperplate print engravings; it also looked as if it was a century old, as old as some bibles were in this house. The writing was also not like the new High German writing. There were times when I had to read passages two or three times before understanding their meanings. This made impressions on me as to what life was supposed to have looked like hundreds of years ago. Although, thinking about the copperplate engravings now, I guess they were perhaps also biased and made to produce certain specific impressions in the viewer's mind, just like most images shown to us today, especially in history and politics.

The year 1944 was for me a year with much fun and pleasant memorable events. This was perhaps mainly due to the fact that I was basically on my own. Outside of the time I spent in school and with school activities I was my own boss. I had to be at the farm at meal times. Otherwise I would not get fed. No one pushed me to do my school work. The farm couple had enough to worry about without having to bother with me. I occasionally kept them informed where I was going, with whom I was with and roughly what we were doing. However, they knew very little of my activities from what I told them. Whenever I was involved in something that was not considered kosher, Tante Herta would find out from neighbours of theirs and then she would tell me not to do that again. I remember being told not to hurl potatoes on a stick like we did. It was easy for us boys to walk around with a stick in our hands and when we got to a farmer's potato pile, and there was one in every farmer's court yard, we only had to pierce a potato and start throwing.

I really got along well with the two Polish girls on the farm. They would teach me quite a few words in Polish. Of course they also fooled me a lot of times. I would try out the new words I learned on the other Polish woman or the girls' mother. The girls at times would wind up getting into just a little bit of trouble with their mother because of the wrong translations they had given me. But their mother also found it funny. These were always words or short sentences of a sexual nature. I suppose I had a good attitude toward the Polish language because my mother spoke fluent Polish. Whenever she came from Hannover I would spring a few new words on her. Even when I tried some of the dirty words on her my mother would not have a problem telling me what they really meant. Often, my mother was also asked by Tante Herta, whether she could come to help with the harvest of a certain crop. And my mother did help because she always got food as compensation. This was better than getting money that she wouldn't have been able to buy anything with anyway. All goods were rationed during the war and everything was in short supply. The black market didn't seem to exist openly, but there actually was some of it. The penalties for dealing in it were probably very harsh. My mother would also come once in a while to do some sewing or fixing of clothes for the farmer. The goods she got to take home would be butter, lard, smoked meat, fruits, vegetables and molasses. What my mother often got was what was in harvest and therefore in greatest supply.

What was on the table in the morning when I had breakfast, when all the others were already working, was mainly bread, molasses and lard. I knew that the workers had a much bigger variety of food on the breakfast table, but I was not jealous, they deserved it. The odd time the meat, sausages and jam were only taken away from the table after I got there; that's how I knew what they had. The coffee everybody drank was 'Ersatzkaffee'. It was a coffee made from ground-up, toasted beet-squares in our area during WWII. In other areas it was also made from roasted acorns, oats, barley and potato peels in some places. To make the brownish water taste better, one could add some chicory. There was no juice, and the milk at the table was for the Ersatzkaffee. The kitchen was just full of flies. There were at least six fly-catcher strips hanging from the ceiling, mainly over the table. The wall above the stove looked black; it was just covered with flies. I still can't imagine what else they could have done to get rid of the flies. Today we would use some sort of fly-poison spray. I was in that same kitchen in 2006, and there were no flies. I suppose with today's use of screens on windows and doors it is much easier to keep the bugs out.

Rationing had been introduced to Germany in late August 1939, shortly before the outbreak of war. For this, stamps were issued to all civilians. Initially most foodstuffs were rationed together with clothing, shoes, leather and soap. The rations were sufficient to live off of, but did not permit luxuries. The ration stamps were colour-coded and covered food like sugar, meat, fruit and nuts, eggs, dairy products, margarine, cooking oil, grains, bread, jams and fruit jellies. Whipped cream became unknown from 1939 until 1948, as well as chocolates, cakes with rich crèmes etc. Meat could not be eaten every day. Other items, such as tropical vegetables and fruits and coffee in particular, were not rationed, but simply became unavailable as they had to be imported from overseas, local vegetables and fruit were not rationed, but only became available when they were harvested. To stretch the flour for bread people were adding ground horse chestnuts, pea meal, potato meal, and barley. Salad spreads were made using chopped herbs mixed with salt and red wine vinegar. Theft of ration stamps or counterfeiting them was a criminal offence and typically resulted in a spell of detention at a forced labour camp. As the war went on it might even have resulted in a death sentence. During the war my mother at times cooked peeled potatoes, mashed them, formed them and then put them into a frying pan. She called them 'Arme Ritter' – poor knights. I guess some of the crusading knights were poor and had little food at times on their marches to and from the Middle East, unless they were plundering. These Arme Ritter, sprinkled with a little sugar were our 'hamburgers'. I actually liked them, but that would be our meal, no fruits or vegetables with it.

As the war began to go against Germany in the Soviet Union and as Allied bombing began to affect domestic production, a more severe rationing program had to be introduced. The system allowed extra rations for men involved in heavy industry, but supplied only starvation rations for Jews and Poles in the areas occupied by Germany. In April 1942, bread, meat and fat rations all were reduced. This was explained to people at the time by poor harvest, lack of manpower for farming, and the increased need to feed the armed forces and the millions of forced labourers and refugees that had come to Germany. Fat was really in short supply all over Germany. The butter rations were very small, perhaps 250 grams per person per month during the last years of the war, 1944/45.

Rationing of consumer goods in Germany started before the war and ended, except for sugar, in 1950 in West Germany and in 1958 for East Germany. In East Germany, rationing of coal stopped only in 1990. The one type of meat Germans, and perhaps a majority of Europeans, have been eating the most, for centuries, is pork. The reason for this is fairly simple. Pigs can be kept near or in the same dwelling with people. They need less room than cows and they eat just about anything. They can eat raw and cooked potatoes and any other vegetables, as well as meat. If there is a mouse or rat in their sty, the pig will catch it and eat it. They will eat all the leftovers from peoples' meals. So they are fairly simple to feed, they don't need the huge pastures that cows are usually kept on. Europe does not have huge areas for grazing cattle; the people are almost sitting in each other's laps. The Netherlands is one of the densest-populated countries in the world. The cows in Europe are basically kept to produce milk and cheese. That is why Europeans are not so crazy about beef; they eat mainly smaller animals. They eat whatever type of animal is best kept in their particular area. In mountainous areas, they eat mutton and lamb. Where horses were used for pulling farm equipment, the horses, when too old to work, were slaughtered and eaten. I have had horsemeat. There is nothing wrong with the meat. For all these reasons the particular type of meat I and many other Germans like is the pork chop. So, in Germany, before the animals were slaughtered, the cows had to get old and the pigs had to get fat. I loved a good slice of rye bread with lard, salt, pepper and onions on it. I must have acquired this from my father; he liked it with a passion.

My mother was always friendly with the Polish women who lived and worked on the farm where I was. The forced- labour people of other nationalities living in this village did get together socially in small groups on Sundays and holidays. They were not allowed to gather out in the open in large groups, but they would visit each other in their rooms in the farm houses they lived in. The largest single nationality was probably the Poles. One day when my mother came to the farm, the Polish mother with the two girls asked my mother to come into her room. She wanted to talk to her. I found out shortly after when my mother explained to Tante Herta what the problem was. The Polish woman had told her that one of her friends just had a child and that the German authorities were going to take the baby away from her in a few weeks when the baby could be weaned off breastfeeding. My mother, after speaking with the farmer where the Polish woman worked and lived, decided to go with the Polish woman to the authorities in the District city and beg them to allow the mother to keep her child. The farmer wrote a note as to how good a worker that Polish mother was, and that it would be easy to bring up the baby on the farm where she was. I'm not a hundred percent sure, but I think that the Schwüblingsen village mayor had also written a note, and the woman was allowed to keep her baby. I should have asked my mother about the mayor, because he was responsible for the village and he was also the guy who wrote the note for my mother to my camp leader to let me leave the camp.

Coming back to the old history books I was studying, I observed that when it comes to making political and historical statements, man has this weird urge not to be totally truthful. By European, especially Christian, measure the crusades were good and honourable events. For that matter, what German history books described about German and European history then was perhaps putting the actions of German tribes or states in a German-biased light. This however is true for any country's history books. What is perhaps the worst thing about this is that the history books are there for the young to learn. The young, without life experiences, don't yet realize that they have to take things with a grain of salt whenever and whatever they read, including and especially history and religious books. Even if they don't remember any details of history, there can be a lifelong impression left with them that foreign people or countries are bad and that their own country always was on the good side of things. The one single item that stuck in my head is the cruelty that was perpetrated by all participating parties during the Thirty-Years' War (1618 – 1648) in Europe.

This religious war between the Catholics and the Protestants, involving every country in central Europe, killed more than one third of the European population. The history book had an engraving showing how the 'Swedish drink' was given. A person was pinned to the ground, spread-eagled, with arms and legs tied to stakes that were driven into the ground. A funnel was then inserted into the person's mouth and liquid manure was poured into the funnel. The person would choke to death on it. This type of torture was called the 'Swedish drink' because it was supposed to have been introduced by the Protestant Swedish troops of King Gustav II, Adolf of Sweden. I imagine, after it was first used by one side, that it was also used later by other sides as well. In this history class we had to memorise our assignments and had to recite portions in class. This is perhaps what made me develop a good habit of memorizing historic events, dates and places.

In spite to the fact that I was placed on this farm to get away from the bombing of Hannover, life in this village was not all that safe either. The village was located only 30 km east of Hannover. Whenever there was a major air-raid on Hannover, I could watch the explosions and fires light up the sky at night. During the daytime the smoke from the fires would darken the sky. These large attacks took place on average once a month with smaller bomb droppings every few days. As early as the beginning of 1944, the Allied air forces were in total control of German air space. From November 1943 on, the bombing of Berlin became a systematic procedure with very few days of no bombing in between. Altogether, there were 389 bombing raids on Berlin, during which 3,823,428 bombs were dropped.

Just about all of the bombers flew over the Gau (the Nazi termi-nology for 'State or Province') Hannover-Braunschweig (the state of Lower Saxony or in German, Niedersachsen). The landscape east and northeast of Hannover, where I was living in 1944, was more or less flat for at least 100 km. The farm houses in the village were low level houses; they only had one floor above ground. The land outside the village was farm land without trees; one could see the horizons far away when outside of the village. For someone that has not seen this it may be hard to visualise. There were some raids in which two thousand planes participated. There were at least three occasions when I lived on this farm during 1944 when I saw the sky filled with planes from horizon to horizon in all directions. The planes would be flying so high that they looked like little, sometimes glittery, silvery specks with vapour trails. It looked beautiful, but we knew what horrific destruction these little specks were about to deliver. When they were flying much lower, one could hear the steady humming of their engines. Whenever they were flying east to deliver their loads to the targets, they would be flying more or less in a formation or at least in nearly equal distance from each other. On their return flight to England they would be a lot more dispersed. Because of that, it would also take a longer time to fly over us. There could be a bunch of fifty or a hundred flying together and often at a much lower altitude.

My mother really had to be in Hannover to look after our home as much as possible. Although it would have been much safer for her on the farm where I was, someone had to be home looking after our belongings. We were so lucky that our house did not get destroyed, when 80 percent of the houses in Hannover were totally destroyed. A study of the bombing was apparently made by 'Rossiwall' in 1966, but it was only entered into the city's archives in 1986. There must have been close to forty to fifty occasions when some or all of the glass in our apartment windows had to be replaced. If someone was not there right away to board up the broken windows after an air raid and protect the inside from the elements, especially during the winter when the weather was wet and miserable, the furniture could be ruined in no time. It also would have been easy for thieves to take advantage of the raids to get into damaged properties and grab whatever pleased them. However, this was just not done. I never heard of a single case where someone had something stolen. I guess the penalty for looting must have been too great. There was also a sort of camaraderie between the people that prevented it from happening.

I also think that the bombings made the German people tougher. It did not break their will to endure it, but it perhaps helped to create some sort of solidarity. During the war, the German war economy actually kept rising until the end of 1944, in spite of the bombings. It is amazing that during the last year of the war one quarter of the population in Germany were foreigners, most of them working to keep the German economy going.

There were also many forced labour camps where the foreigners were treated terribly and many died during the war, a lot of them of starvation. However, ordinary Germans only found out about this after the war.

To keep the Germans' spirit up in the last year of the war, there were also announcements made by the Nazis that Germany had 'Vergeltungswaffen', weapons that would be coming out soon which would turn the war around. These announcements were half-believed, but the majority of Germans were also hoping that they were true. After all, the German population was suffering tremendously. The German V1 and V2 rockets that hit London in the last few months of the war were supposed to be the beginning of what the German Propaganda Ministry said was still coming. The 'V' abbreviation stood for the German word 'Vergeltung', meaning revenge. Of course we found out after the war that there were no other weapons coming, those were just promises that helped to keep up the peoples' will to endure and continue fighting.

My mother would come to the farm perhaps once in four to six weeks. Whenever she came, she would stay for a couple of days and if the farmer needed her help badly enough she would stay for four or five days. For me it was perhaps a time that toughened me. The year before, in the camp in 1943, at age eleven, I was more or less on my own. I had no one to go and talk to, but in that I was treated just like everyone else. None of the other boys had a grownup to go to either, to open up to and get sympathy from. In that camp the boys developed some sort of camaraderie; we learned to stick together and help each other. The grownups were considered the side from which the real trouble could come. We had to be on guard against that side. However, on this farm in 1944, at age twelve, I felt totally on my own. I had no one to go to and confide in. With the friends I made I did not have exactly the same relations as with the boys in the camp. The farmer's wife was not a person I could go to, she had two boys of her own who were younger and who she treated like her kids. And why not, they were her kids.

However, I was also still a kid, yet I was treated like I was living in a hotel as a grownup. The *hotel* had a timetable that I had to abide by; I got no preferential treatments as a kid, although the other two boys got away with murder. I knew my place and I understood the situation. I did not even tell my mother how I felt and what bothered me. She would not have been able to do anything about it, I figured, and she had plenty of her own problems to worry about. My mother was glad and grateful that I had a place to stay, with enough food, and did not have to be in Hannover. I did not want to burden my mother with the little problems I had. I think I already understood then that my life could be so much worse in comparison to others. My sister was still in the Harz Mountains, near the place she was in 1942. My mother still had to see her once in a while, although she did not go as frequently as before. Where my sister was in the mountain, she was relatively safe from the bombings.

The air raid shelter we had on this farm was a trench in the ground about twenty feet long, not more than seven feet wide and seven feet deep. Over the trench were logs across the width with about three feet of dirt on top. It just looked like a little three-foot high hill in the fruit tree garden in back of the farmhouse, but 200 feet away from it. The entrance was a sort of a dirt ramp at a forty-five-degree angle at one end of the trench. At the bottom of the ramp was a wooden door to keep the weather out. This shelter could barely stop heavy aircraft machine gun fire let alone save us from bombs. I guess it was mainly to get away from the farmhouse which was a more likely target. We all, the farm family, the foreigners on the farm and I, had to fit into this mud hole, at least that's what it was when it was raining. During the daytime many of the working people on the farm were outside the village working the fields, especially in the spring, summer and fall. When there were air raids during the day it was mainly us kids, Tante Herta and her mother-in-law that went into this shelter.

I often saw some of the results of the air raids on Hannover, where my mother was. In a straight line, we were only perhaps 20 km away from Hannover. So I could see the western horizon covered with smoke during the daytime and all lit up by the burning houses during the night. It would always take one, two or three weeks before I found out that my mother was still alive, people did not have telephones like today. The outskirt closest to us, east of Hannover was Misburg, it had a big oil refinery. Whenever this place was bombed, one could see the smoke and fires especially well. It was always worrisome for me because where my mother lived was also east from the centre of Hannover, and I did not know which area was hit. It was only hours later that the news over the radio would give an indications of what sections of the city were hit. However, to not discourage the German population, the number of dead and the amount of damage given was always kept fairly low. At times there were also heavy bombings, when no incendiary bombs were dropped and very few fires and smoke were created. However, the destruction caused by the heavy bombings was just as horrific. At this time the Allies were already dropping several different types of blockbusters bombs, some of them weighing 12,000 pounds. The Grand Slam was a 22,000 pound (10,000 kg) earthquake bomb used by RAF Bomber Command.

This was the Oil Refinery at Misburg just east of Hannover. It was bombed several times, as a result I could see the smoke during the day and fire at night.

The German radio communication system was excellent during the war; telling the people where the Allied planes were, how many, in what directions they were flying, what the most likely targets were, then what the actual targets were, when the planes were on their way home and whether they thought it was safe to leave the shelters. Often the tracking system was also fooled, when, for example, a thousand or more planes bombarded Berlin or Madeburg and in reality dropped only part of their loads. On the way home they would then drop their remaining bombs on one or more unexpected targets. This happened to Hannover quite often, because it was on route to and from Berlin.

In this little farm village we also had two close calls. About 3 km in a straight line east from our village was an oil refinery just outside the village of Dollbergen. This refinery was bombed twice while I was in Schwüblingsen during the summer of 1944. The first attack must have consisted of hundreds of planes. It was during the day. We were at our dirt shelter, standing at the entrance ramp and watching the planes fly overhead. We, mainly the adults, were wondering what target they had in mind, when all of a sudden the ground started to shake and we started to hear the explosions of bombs come closer and closer. We got into the shelter in a flash and pulled the wooden entrance door closed. At one point I was sure that we would get hit as well. The area around the oil refinery was carpet bombed. The dirt seeping through the log cracks in the shelter's roof must have raised the floor's level by at least a half an inch.

The whole raid lasted for about an hour before it started to quiet down. When we got out of our crouched positions, we shook off the dirt from ourselves. The closest bombs hit the fields only a few hundred feet from us. There was only one farm between the farm I was on, and the eastern end of the village. Not one bomb fell in the village, yet the fields within a 3 km radius of the oil refinery were honeycombed with craters. Some bombs fell just outside of our village. Many people were working the fields and some got killed. In one case they found a crater which contained a wagon, two dead horses and the driver. He was one of the prisoners of war, living on a farm as a farm worker. The craters were big enough to drop in a small bungalow. We could see and smell the black smoke from the burning oil refinery for many days after. The same refinery was bombed a second time but this time the bombs were more or less concentrated on the facility itself.

Just to show what carpet-bombing looks like – This was an Oil refinery in Hamburg which was carpet-bombed

The railway line going past our village about half a kilometre away was also the main line to Berlin and the eastern part of Germany. Often, the Allied fighter planes, having accompanied their bombers to their targets, would, flying very low, attack anything that moved on the ground. Any time there was a train in sight it would get strafed with heavy-explosive type machine-gun fire. Just about every railroad crossing had manned barriers. The crossings would have little houses beside them in which the operators lived. Any time there were enemy planes in the area, these barrier attendances would go into their little shelters. The shelters were often one-man concrete shelters with steel doors. They were just standing above ground a little distance away from the houses. I guess that unless they took a direct hit, a man could survive in them, a little tossed around, but alive. The crossing guard closest to our village even had his family living with him in the railway barrier-house. One time this fellow was caught outside and was shot at. He got hit in the rear end and suffered a fairly big wound. We kids often found some of these large fighter-plane machine-gun bullets; they were almost one half inch in diameter. They were supposed to be handed in imme-diately, however, we always kept the best or the oddest deformed-looking ones.

Some of the fun times I had on the farm included harvesting time. That would be when the weather was the hottest and when my mother was always asked to come and help. They would harvest wheat, rye, barley and oats in a big way. It was late summer and no school. The whole farm was alive. The staff would get up at sunrise and work until sunset. In spite of the workers basically being prison-ers of war and forced labourers from Poland, Ukraine and Belgium, there was a sort of spirit as if it was one family working together.

I would also get up earlier than getting up for school. It was my job to carry the food for the breaks to the field. The food was a little better than normal too. After all, these people worked hard. They had breakfast in the farmhouse after they got up. Then there was a nine or ten o'clock break in the field, twelve to one lunch time in the field, and another break at three o'clock. Supper was maybe at seven, at the farmhouse. I was sometimes asked to take one of the horses back to the farm. They had five horses, and two were of a type called Belgians. They were big workhorses. They looked like the ones in today's beer commercials, pulling wagons loaded with beer barrels. These Belgians were gentle horses. They were powerful but easy going. The other three looked more like well-fed race horses. They were also big and strong but they were much more lively and fidgety. The worst was the youngest, a beautiful brown-haired beast. Actually, they were all brown. They were giants to me, a little twelve-year-old. The horses were never abused by anyone. After they had worked for a while in the field, they would be allowed to rest. At times I was asked to take a horse back to the stable. This could be a little over 1km walk from the field to the village.

After a couple of times walking these horses back I asked if I could ride a horse. There was no saddle or anything to hold on to accept the horse's mane, but there was a bridle. The heavy Belgian horses were easy to handle. They just walked the whole way. The Ukrainian would lift me onto a horse's back and slap the horse on its hind quarters. The horses knew their way all by themselves, all I had to do was hold on to them. The last one I rode was the youngest, the two-or-three-year old. It went pretty well at the beginning, but as we got closer to the village the horse went into a little trot. The closer we got the faster the trot became. The farm village had a sort of an oval main road and one road through the middle of the long diameter of the oval. The farm houses were located on both sides of these two roads.

When we got to the village we had to make a right turn onto the oval ring road, then a left-turn onto the road going through the middle of the village. From this intersection, about 400 feet further, was the entrance to the farm courtyard. Well, this young horse put a good scare into me rounding the first turn at a good clip. Now we were in the village and almost home when the pace still kept increasing. By the time we got to the second, the left turn, the horse must have thought it was in a derby. It felt to me like the horse was making that turn on the spot. I just flew, like a bullet launched from a catapult, off the horse. It must have been the speed with which I went through the air that saved me from landing on the cobblestone road. I landed instead in the much softer grass covered ditch.

No one saw me. The landing wasn't bad, I felt some pain, but where was the horse? I got up and ran like crazy the 400 feet along the garden fence and the huge hay barn. It felt like forever to get to the farm-courtyard entrance. When I got to the gate, I saw the horse standing in front of the horse stable door looking at me as if to ask me 'where were you?' I opened the stable door and it walked right in, and I with it. I then had to tie the horse onto a line in its proper spot. The horses knew the exact location where they were always tied up. I then went to the front part to put water and feed into the troughs. I think this is what made the horse run, it was thirsty and hungry. I really liked going into the horse stable. I liked the odour in the place. I would even chew some of the horses' feed. Beside the hay, they got some grain, oats and there were little pieces like cornflakes, I believe they were made from dried sugar-beets. These pieces tasted sweet and just a little bit like liquorice. We kids would chew at least a couple every time we were in the stable.

It just struck me how the farm house and stables were physically located. All the buildings were connected. One could walk from the farmer's living quarters within the main buildings to all the stables without having to go outside. The closest to the farmer's living space were the rooms of the farm help, at this time occupied by the foreigners. Isn't it ironic – in order for these people to communicate with each other they spoke German; it was the only language they had in common? The Ukrainian and the Polish women and girls could scrape by using some of the words that Ukrainian and Polish had in common. Coming back to the buildings, the next closest was the horse stable, and then the large cow stalls and the farthest were the pigsties. However, the pigsty was the most visited by everyone. It had this long corridor with windows on the left and about ten pigsties on the right. The toilet was half way down with the pigsties right and left. The human waste went into the same underground piping system as the pigs' waste, as well as the horses' and cows' liquid waste. They had a 'Jauchewagen' a wagon with a wooden drum that could hold perhaps 3,000 litres of liquid manure. The liquid was collected in a holding tank that must have been located under the cobblestone courtyard. The liquid was pumped out through a manhole right beside the main entrance to the farm house.

There was no shortage of smells on this farm. It seemed every third week or so the manure was spread on some of the many cow pastures they had. During the summer most of the cows were out in one of the pastures and were constantly rotated from pasture to pasture to allow the pastures to recover. They had enough pasture land to enable them to cut grass as well, to make hay for the winter months when the cows were kept in the stables.

Coming back to our toilet, it was just a three foot wide, two foot deep horizontal board to sit on with a hole in the middle. The front part below the seat was a vertical board that went right across the three-foot width of the space. It was like a bench with a hole in it that was set into a three foot deep closet against the back wall. The walls of this closet were only about four and a half feet high, the same as the pigsty walls. There was no door in front. It was just wide open. When a grownup stood at the entrance of the pigsty he could see right over the top of all the sties and the toilet. This is where all the people on the farm had to go when the need arose. People on the farm had no trouble with this. They didn't know better. In bad weather this was much better than the 'Donnerbalken', the thunder-log in the camp I was at the year before.

Today, I guess most city-type women would throw up if they had to go to a strong-manure-like smelling toilet like this was. The pigs were farting, grunting and sometimes squealing when they were fighting. The roof beams and posts holding up the red terracotta-shingled roof were covered with spider webs, as dense and dusty as one would expect to see in a Hollywood horror movie castle. When one was sitting on this throne, one would be totally in view of anyone standing in front of the stall. The standard procedure when sitting there would be to listen for someone entering the pigsty corridor and then make some sort of noise to announce that the toilet was busy. Everyone had their peculiar ways of announcing their presence. Some would simple call "busy," some would whistle and some would call "who is it?"

The toilet paper we used was just newspaper, there was no other paper. This paper then wound up in the same holding tank as manure and wound up as solid waste that was eventually taken to rot in the fields and become fertiliser for the fields on which wheat, barley, rye and potatoes etc. grew. To think of it, this farm, as well as all the people in the farm village, did not produce any garbage. There was no waste to be taken away. The society we have today is a consumer society. Our society collapses if we stop consuming. However, our consumption is also what kills all the other species on earth. Per capita Canada produces the most garbage in the world. This year, 2018, China decided not to take our garbage any more. What are Homo sapiens doing to this world?

On route to the pigsty one had to go through what they called the 'Waschküche', the laundry-room. The German word 'Waschküche', translated literally, means the kitchen in which the washing is done. The room was about twelve by twelve feet. It had doors to the main house, the courtyard and the pigsty. Against one brick wall with a big chimney was a large cauldron with a large fireplace underneath. This huge kettle was never allowed to rest, it had many diverse usages. I think it was every second Monday that everyone's wash was done in this tub. It could hold perhaps eighty litres of liquid. When the wash was done, the whole room became more like a steam bath. Twice a year, the cauldron was used to make soap. Soap was a very rare, hard-to-get item in Germany during the war. However, this farmer had no trouble making it, it was made mainly from fat and I believe they also used the bones of pigs they had slaughtered. They would boil the crap out of it all, add caustic soda and I don't know what else. It seemed to be a long process, but it was good soap, especially when it could be used for trading.

In late summer, when the sugar beets were harvested, the whole Waschküche became a little syrup factory. The large sugar beets were cut small and then crushed. The crushed pulp was then put into a large screw-type press. The juice coming out, looking and tasting like sweet water was poured into the cauldron. It was then boiled for hours and hours, until most of the water was boiled away and the leftover was a thick, sweet, dark brown syrup. It was molasses. I don't know if they made more than one cauldron-full of syrup, but the cooking seemed to go on for days. It smelled up the whole place. Once the process was over there was enough to last for us fifteen or so people for the rest of the year. I was not tempted to take any of this syrup while it was being made, because I got my fill of it at breakfast and sometimes lunchtime.

It is amazing how often people get food poisoning today. We, today, must have become too sensitive. On this farm, the milk we drank came directly from the cows, it was not pasteurized. There were no fridges or freezers in ordinary households. Sometimes the milk curdled when it was added to the coffee. When the milk went sour, it was put aside, and it became cheese that one spread on a slice of bread, or ate with boiled potatoes. If a solid type, Edam for example, would become mouldy or get worms, like in the camp, the worms were removed, or the mould was cut off and the cheese was eaten. Sometimes the bread was mouldy, it was then given to the pigs, and they ate everything. We always ate in the kitchen. It must have had thousands of flies. The food around the table always had flies landing on it. One got sort of used to this. In those days, houses were not equipped with window screens like they are today. It was also not hard to find spiders in the corners of the rooms. They were catching the odd fly in their webs. I think we have become too isolated from the rest of the creatures on earth. That is perhaps why we think we can live without them. If we don't destroy ourselves, nature will do it for us. One day, nature may present us with a blow that we never anticipated, and consequently can't recover from.

Coming back to the pigsty, what I did like to eat on my way to and from the toilet were boiled potatoes. The same cauldron was also used to boil potatoes for the pigs. The farmer had a special sieve that would allow sorting the potatoes. The small potatoes would fall through the sieve to become solely food for the pigs. This farmer produced truckloads of potatoes. The larger ones we ate, but the majority were sold. At that time, in our area, people did not eat potatoes with the skin, or at least not very often. These small potatoes for the pigs were not peeled. However, the pigs had no trouble eating them with the peel. I guess, at that time, no one had discovered yet that the vitamins, on most fruits and vegetables, are just under the skin. Unless the cauldron was used for washing or boiling molasses, or making soap, it was used every day for boiling potatoes. Whenever I had to go to the toilet I would grab a few of these small potatoes out of the cauldron on the way to and from the toilet. I loved to eat these pigs' potatoes, most of them were much smaller than a ping-pong ball; they tasted better than the peeled giants I got on my dinner plate. The skins were so thin and smooth; no wonder the pigs liked them. These potatoes, when well cooked and still fairly hot, melted in my mouth, they were like a dessert to me.

Talking about food, another thing I learned eating on this farm was to take a fresh egg, punch a hole in both ends and suck the inside out through one of the holes. To most people this would not look too appetising, but I loved it. It is not really that tasty when done with old eggs.

Another thing I remember about the harvest of rye, which was perhaps the grain that was seeded the most, to make rye-bread, was catching rabbits. The crops were rotated every year so that the soil had a better chance to stay rich in nutrients; every crop has its specific demands on the soil. This year, the rye was sown on the piece of land the farmer owned along the railway tracks, next to the railway crossing. The farmers there had fields all over the place, some fields close by and others far away from the village. I guess that sort of fractured land ownership came from buying up pieces of land when some farmer family got out of the business, but perhaps mainly through the type of marriages they got into. The kids would mainly marry other close-by farm kids, perhaps from a close-by village. The parents would then split up their land holdings for the kids, so that the kids could stay in the area. Some of the land of the farm I lived on was from the wife's side and some from the husband's side.

Near the railway crossing-barrier operator's house was a sort of a sand pit. This sandpit had a few holes that had families of hares living in them. I guess they also ate rye or perhaps some other plants that were growing within the fields. As the reaping machine was being pulled through the fields to harvest the grain there were always some hares that would jump out of the field in front of the machine. We kids were encouraged to chase the hares, who were always faster than we were. However, two or three times, during the couple of days we harvested near the sandpit, the Ukrainian would get involved and corner the hares. He then clubbed a couple to death with a sort of truncheon. Someone took them back to the farmhouse right away and they became our meat for supper. As a kid I found nothing wrong with that kind of catching animals; however, today I would loudly protest against it. I have changed.

Live and let live. Now I feel there is no need for the killing sports – hunting and fishing – in our industrialized societies.

As the grain was cut down, by the large two-horse drawn mower, it was automatically tied into fairly equal-sized bundles and left lying on the ground. People then had to stand up the bundles in stacks, leaning against each other in a sort of upside down V form. There would be perhaps ten bundles placed together. These stacks, about fifteen feet apart, would stand there for a week or more, depending on the amount of rainfall, until they were really dry. The grain was then loaded onto hay wagons which were pulled by two or four horses depending how hard or soft the soil was. The wagons were loaded up to between eleven and twelve feet high above the ground. On the paved road, two horses had no trouble pulling these wagons to the farmhouse. It was good for the farmer to have five horses; they could easily be alternated so that they got some rest once in a while. In the farm courtyard the grain was threshed, the kernels were removed from the chaff and the leftover straw was again bundled. The straw was then stacked up to the roof of the first large barn. That straw was used to cover the floors of the cow, horse and pig stables. The husk and a little of the straw were also cut up very fine and mixed with the oats for the horses and the grain for the cows during the winter.

This harvesting required a lot of people. Some people had to load the wagons in the field, some to take the wagons to the farmhouse, some had to operate the thresher and some to move and stack the straw in the barn. My mother was always asked to help but there were also people from other farmers that would come over to help. This was always a two to three-day affair. For me it was almost like a party. Whenever the work was hard, there was a noticeable improvement in the type of food that was served, more meat and better sandwich spreads. It was amazing how people helped each other, and the majority were not even Germans. But our farm-help also had to go and help at other farmers at times.

As the Allied armies got closer to Germany, there were also Nazis of foreign nationalities that came to Germany with the hope that Germany would still win the war. According to some reports the Nazi friendly Dutch cooperated more closely with the Nazis than the people in any other country. This may come as a surprise to a lot of people. There were even Dutch SS troops fighting the Russian troops in Berlin in the last days of the war, according to some reports and Wikipedia. I saw a lecture of a Dutch/Canadian architect, who is also a Jew, being asked "why the Dutch, of all the Germany occupied countries, seemed to hate the Germans the most." His reply was "It is because of their guilt feelings."

In the fall of 1944, my farmer was asked to put up a Dutch couple. They were perhaps in their late thirties. They told me that they were teachers and didn't want to live in Holland with the American troops that were coming to enter Holland. They were very nice people, always well dressed. They never had to do any work and spoke very good German with a Dutch accent. It sounded a little funny to me when they talked. They acted like hotel guests. They seemed to have a special interest in me. They talked to me quite a bit; they didn't tell me, but I think they felt sorry for me.

One day, it must have been in early November of 1944, my mother came to visit me for a couple of days, or perhaps do something for Tante Herta, I don't remember which. On the second day these people talked to my mother while I was in school. When I came home, I noticed that my mother had been crying. My mother then took me up to my room and asked me if what the Dutch people had told her was true. They told her that I was treated by Tante Herta like a 'Stiefkind', a stepchild, that is, I was not treated in a nice way, which was true.

This was a fairly well-off farmer. Compared to city people or small farmers, they had plenty during the war. I guess I was not worse off than the foreign workers who were on this farm. But the Dutch couple noticed that the two farmer's sons got special treatments and that I, as a twelve-year-old, had more restraints and was not treated like an equal kid. At breakfast I always had to watch the sons getting their slices of bread prepared by their mother with special spreads on them. It could have been meat, sausage spreads, cheese or marmalade on butter. I had to make my own slices, using what was put on the table for me, that was bread, lard and sugar-beet syrup. But what really hurt me was that the sons got cookies and I had to watch the boys eating them. About every Saturday, early in the morning, Tante Herta would make dough to bake bread at the village's bakery. Every once in a while she also made some special wheat dough and took it to the baker to bake loafs of bread that were about six inches wide, two inches high and eighteen inches long. Perhaps between 9:00 and 10:00 a.m. she would go and pick up the baked loaves. At home she would slice these loafs into half-inch-thick slices. She would then put a sugar glaze on half of them and on the other half a chocolate glaze. I have no idea where she got the chocolate from.

Chocolate was one of the rarest treats Germans could hope to get, which happened maybe once a year, at Christmas. During the war, chocolate was reserved for soldiers, but mainly for air force pilots. Before noon, Tante Herta would then take the covered slices back to the baker to slowly dry the glaze. When she picked up the three 1.5 by 2 foot trays in the afternoon, with these glazed biscuits, she would carry them right away into the house. Shortly after, she would come out of the house, whenever she knew her sons were around, and give them a couple each of the sugar- and chocolate-glazed biscuits. Sometimes the three of us would be playing in the front courtyard and Tante Herta, coming back from the baker with the trays, would see us together. However, normally when she came out of the house she would only call her boys and give them cookies and I went empty handed. I don't know whether the boys were told that this treat was for them only. Nevertheless, I could only watch them eat.

The reader may think 'how terrible,' to do this to a child. Yet how different is this from having the poor watch the rich indulge themselves? Is this not already the basic start of what is wrong with our societies? Why must we make such distinctions between next of kin, or friends and strangers? It is understandable when animals make that distinction because they only do it with the food that they have for that day, they don't hoard. Humans for some reason must hoard. There are untold numbers of individuals who pile up enough wealth that could otherwise allow hundreds of people to spent more than one hundred thousand dollars each year for every year of their lives. It is this grand-scale accumulation that is doing perhaps the greatest harm to this planet.

We, the average individuals from North America and Europe, often go on expensive vacation trips to the poorer countries around the world. There, we can walk by starving, poor begging children without giving them a cent. Yet, shortly after seeing them we may walk into fine, expensive restaurants and splurge on the finest food and drinks that that country has to offer. We have all kinds of excuses for our behaviour. Why could our Western corporations, employing children in some countries, paying as little as six cents to make a whole shirt, not employ the parents of the children and pay them sixty cents per shirt? This would perhaps allow the children to go to school. After all, the shirts may get sold for fifty dollars in North America.

Coming back to the biscuits, I only got one or two of those slices on Sunday afternoons for coffee. This was also when the foreigners got their treats. Tante Herta also made flans with a sugar coating at the baker's. Or, whenever one of the many types of fruit they had was ripe, some flans would be covered with fruit. Getting pieces of these flans was also reserved for Sundays, unless Tante Herta wanted to get rid of them more quickly. This would happen every now and then. The food was stored in a pantry which was located in the main house and locked. However, once in a while, mice managed to get in there and do their thing – eat and leave droppings. A major pantry clean-up by Tante Herta would then take place. She tried to find out how they got in there and set traps.

But more often the sugar flans were invaded by ants. When this happened, we often got the sugar and fruit flans as treats during the week and we were told that they had to go. We all knew what that meant; watch out for the ants that are still in or around the flans. It was not a big problem for us. I guess today most people in the western world, especially city people, are so far removed from nature that they would throw flans like that into the garbage. The kitchen on this farm was the place where we all ate every day, except the farm family would eat in their living room on Sundays. This room was locked during the week so that it could not be used by anyone and would stay clean.

CHAPTER TEN
RETURNING TO HANNOVER – TILL THE END OF THE WAR

When I confirmed, that what my mother was told by the Dutch couple was correct, and that it did bother me a little, my mother confronted Tante Herta. At the end of her conversation with Tante Herta my mother decided to take me back to Hannover with her. She did not want me to live like that. There was no big fight, and my mother and the farmer were still friends. It was near the end of November 1944.

By that time, it was about six months before the end of the war, some rules in Germany had started to become more flexible or less important. My mother was able to take me back to Hannover without any objections from the school or the village's mayor. However, the bombing of Hannover had also tremendously escalated by this time. On the way to Hannover, my mother told me what the daily routine was. The biggest item was how to deal with the now almost daily air raid alarms. There were no more functioning schools in Hannover, so that was one item I didn't have to bother with. The same applied to the Jungvolk meetings, no more of those. The air-raid sirens were wailing almost daily, which made the less essential activities more or less unworkable. To find out in which stores food was available, where and how far one could move within the city to be close enough to an air-raid shelter, were two of the biggest considerations we had to think about.

When I entered Hannover again, after being away from it for two years, I saw what the bombing had done to it during that period. Large housing blocks in our neighbourhood were totally destroyed, whereas in some places only one house within a row of five or six was down. To my amazement today, our rectangular block, consisting of about twenty, four- to-five-storey houses, was still intact up to this point. The wailing of sirens was much more important to pay attention to here in the city than on the farm. The cities were important targets. I was only home a day or two when we had to run to the bunker that was located at the Welfenplatz. This was the bunker that I watched being constructed during the beginning of the war. I went into it a few times before going to the camp in 1943, but at that time a lot of people still took shelter in their own houses' cellars. Now no one dared stay home. The bunker was often packed; we were like sardines in a can.

Otto's Bunker in Hannover in 1944 - capacity 10,000. This picture was taken during trip to Germany in 1960. At that time it was being used as a hotel.

Everyone was assigned to a room from the beginning. According to its size and shape, a room could easily have been a jail cell, except it had no door or window. The room was about six feet wide, eleven feet long and seven feet high. Around the walls were benches, which were meant for women, the elderly and children when it was crowded. After a while, one got to know pretty-well everyone in the room. By this time, after five years of war already, there were no more overweight people around. Yet one woman still sticks in my mind and that is a woman who was constantly complaining about everything. She was the only one that was a little on the heavy side. What perhaps may have enabled her to get more food than the normal person was the fact that she was a party member. She had some sort of black uniform with a party member button on the lapel. However, she was with us for only about a month. Maybe she didn't get enough sympathy from our people and went to try her luck at some other room.

Back in Hannover, one of my scariest air raids was on November 26th, 1944 when 1,100 B-24 heavy bombers, accompanied by 700 fighter planes, attacked the oil refinery at Misburg. This place is located just at the outskirts east of Hannover, in a straight line about 7 km from where I lived. Up to this point, this refinery had already been bombed about a dozen times. I witnessed some of these from 25 km away when I was in Schwüblingsen, never knowing whether the area where my mother lived was involved. Our bunker was filled with people way above its capacity and according to peoples' speculations, these bombs could have been falling anywhere. This was also sort of a milestone for the Allies bombers because it was pretty well the last time that Germany could muster some sort of fighter air defence. The German Luftwaffe launched about 200 fighter planes, of which at least 112 were shot down. The Americans also lost a number of planes, but for Germany it was devastating.

One of the most important things to pay attention to at that time was the radio. It was switched on at our place just about all the time, day and night. Of course, there were the sirens that would wail short sounds for advanced warning, continuous high- and low-pitched wailing for warning, long low-pitched sounds as an advanced clear signal and a continuous low-pitched sound as the all-clear signal. But, as already mentioned, on the radio there was a frequency that continuously broadcast what was going on in the skies in terms of attacking enemy planes. They would inform us whenever foreign planes were approaching German air space, how many, what type of bomber and/or fighter planes they were, what direction they were flying and what the possible targets could be. Already, from the beginning of the war, we had the radio antenna connected to the lead sheath of our incoming telephone cable, as mentioned earlier. People were told to connect their radio antennas to these telephone lead sheaths if there was one reachable. I'm not sure whether they transmitted the signal over this lead-cable-cover or whether the lead sheath just made a better antenna. The latter, in a way, does not seem to make sense, because I assume the sheath must also have been grounded. However, it worked.

By this time I was twelve and a half years old and a little more knowledgeable and curious about politics, especially in what direction the war was going in. The German news broadcasts were still talking of winning the war. They were still talking about the secret weapons Germany had, and that those weapons would turn our fortunes around soon. One indication of how desperate the German situation was becoming was perhaps the use of voluntary suicide missions. The Germans had come up with manned torpedoes in the English Channel to sink Allied ships. One type allowed the pilots to bail out before hitting, whereas in the second type the pilot stayed inside and perished. However, the ones that could bail out normally did not survive either. The idea was that the pilot could steer the torpedo to the target from a much farther distance than unmanned torpedoes.

The last time we had heard from my father was several months earlier, from the Russian front in the east. The Germans had been retreating with heavy losses for months. My sister was still in Hohegeiss in the Harz Mountains; we had not heard from her for a while but considered her quite safe where she was. In our bunker room there were rumours that someone, no one knew who, had heard something over the radio about how things were going for Germany. These comments were coming from the BBC's broadcasts in German and from the Voice of America in German. Some people would brush this off as propaganda, very seldom would someone openly put any credence into what one heard, they had to be one-hundred percent sure that the person they spoke to was like-minded. Even my mother was not completely sure about me. She would not say anything against the Nazis to me.

One day, curiosity got the better of me and when my mother was not in the house I started tuning the radio to one of the foreign German-speaking broadcasts. I think to get better normal radio reception I disconnected the antenna from the lead telephone sheath. What got me hooked on the Voice of America was not the talking but the music. The Nazis always called American Jazz pure evil. Germans were not allowed to listen to it, let alone own records of American music. So I had never heard this type of music before.

The biggest thing was the music of Glen Miller. I had a hard time keeping the volume down or, worse, shutting it off.

I think it was a day shortly after Christmas 1944 when my mother caught me listening to the BBC news. She asked me what I was doing and told me that it is against the law to listen to any foreign station. I told her that I liked the American music and that this was between us, we just don't tell anyone about it. She told me then that she had been listening to the foreign broadcasts for quite a while, long before I came back to Hannover, but that she was afraid to tell me. Kids have gotten their parents into big trouble, even though it was mostly unintentional. Kids would tell someone something and a third party would overhear it and report it to the authorities. The Nazis had vehicles, like vans, with radio direction antennas mounted on top of the roof. These looked like round loops that could be rotated 360 degrees. There would be a man sitting inside the van watching an instrument telling him what frequency the antenna was picking up. This was mainly used to pick up spies broadcasting messages, but it also worked, over a short range, on picking up the frequency that a radio was tuned to.

I found out later, as a teenager, when I was building my own radios, that the tube type radio also transmitted, although faintly, as part of its operation, the carrier frequency it was tuned to. We only had this 'Volksempfänger,' the type of radio that Hitler had ordered to be built early on in his reign. It was to be designed cheaply so that every German could afford one. There were actually three sizes – small, medium and big. Ours was a medium. These radios worked well, I wonder how many of them were used to work against Hitler? These radios were used, in addition to warning the population about enemy aircraft activities over Germany, also as a propaganda tool to keep up the spirit of the German people. At the beginning of the war it was mainly to heighten their enthusiasm for war and at the end it was to scare people about what the enemy would do to them after they have given up the fight.

The atrocities committed by the Russian troops against the fleeing Germans in the East were talked about daily. The single biggest loss of life was the sinking of the hospital ship Wilhelm Gustloff on January 30, 1945 by a Soviet submarine. It was packed with about 10,500 people, mainly women and children refugees trying to escape from near Danzig, East Prussia. About 9,400 people were supposed to have lost their lives. It is the biggest sea disaster ever in history. The Russian sub was waiting in the Baltic Sea in front of the harbour so it could sink the ship after it left the port. Poland actually made a documentary film of this event, which the BBC, I believe it was, used to elaborate on in more detail.

From January 1945 on, the air-raid alarms became almost a daily thing to live with. It could be any time of the day or night when we had to run to the bunker. The British attacked at night and the Americans during the day. Most often these alarms involved enemy planes flying nearby or over Hannover but actually attacking other places. One never knew when or where bombs would drop on Hannover. When bombs dropped on Hannover, often other parts of the city were hit and the only thing affecting us was that we could feel the ground shaking. This shaking was transmitted to us through the building structure. We tried to judge by the intensity whether the bombs were coming closer. Often the power would go off, even when only other parts of the city were hit. Some emergency lights would then come on because the bunker had an emergency power plant that would normally be started up after a few minutes.

The bunker was designed to hold 10,000 people but by now it was often overfilled. To keep the ventilation going when the Hydro power was off, there were rooms with manual fans on every floor at both ends. The fans were such that a person would be sitting and, instead of having pedals for the feet, there were horizontal handles at chest height in front of them, these had to be turned continuously. Only capable men, although there were not that many, and young women had to perform this duty. Often when the power was off they did it in the dark. Many times even the emergency power did not work either. Overall the emergency system did seem to work very well. At times there was a lot smoke outside the bunker, but because of filters the air inside was breathable. We would often leave the bunker when the air outside was filled with smoke from houses that were burning a kilometre or more away from us. But we had to go home to see whether our house was still standing, and whether something had to be done to the doors and windows.

Hannover had already had several major attacks before I came back home. However, the first major attack I experienced at the beginning of 1945 was of our city district, it was during the night. It began as an attack with incendiary bombs and lasted several hours. After everything was burning, they came and dropped explosive bombs. It was about 10:00 in the morning when the all-clear signal came, telling us that we could go home. People were slowly leaving but some would also come back in, saying they could not stand the smoke outside. My mother and I stayed put for at least half an hour after the all clear signal was given. As mentioned earlier, the bunker had one floor below ground level, one at ground level and one floor above the ground level. There were only three entrances to get into and out of this bunker, one at each end at ground level and one in the centre facing the plaza. The centre entrance was meant for the first floor. One had to climb up about sixteen concrete steps on the outside of the bunker to get to a little concrete platform from which one could enter the first floor level. This entrance also had two thick steel doors, with a little vestibule in between them. We liked to use this entrance because our room was located on the first floor, not too far from the entrance. This way we didn't have to squeeze past all the people in the inside corridors and stairs, which we had to do a few times when we had entered through one of the two ground floor entrances. People had to have a lot of patience.

As we started to move through the corridor toward the upper exit/entrance, we started to hear people coughing and moaning. When I stepped from the vestibule onto the platform, I got a horrific picture burned into my memory that I can always recall. Wherever I turned my head, I saw red. I could not see any further than perhaps a hundred feet. The whole place looked like bright reddish smoke. All the housing blocks on three sides of the bunker were ablaze, but I could not see them. However, I could feel the heat, even though the closest were about 300 feet away from the bunker. By the time we left the bunker the fires had already burned for hours. By now pretty well only the outside walls of these four- and five-storey houses were still partially standing. The floors, which were mainly of wood, together with the apartments' furniture and contents, had fallen into the inside, providing material for intensely hot bonfires.

Through luck again, only the direction in which we had to go to our house was passable. In all the other three directions of the bunker, the houses and the old solidly brick-built, huge army barracks were burning. We were walking briskly, with burning throats and eyes, toward the side that wasn't red, although smoke-filled, in the direction towards our house. It took at least ten minutes before we turned the last corner to get a glimpse at our house in the distance. The whole side of the housing block, which our house was roughly in the middle of, was still standing. There were some isolated houses that were burning nearby, but the brunt of this major firestorm-type attack was more in a westerly and southerly direction from our bunker, covering an area of about four to five square kilometres. It took three or four days before fires were out and everything was more or less under control again. Luckily our house was spared once more.

Another time, after one of the several-hours stays in the bunker, during which mainly other districts were bombed, my mother and I decided to leave the bunker before the all-clear signal was given. From the vibrations during the raid we knew that a few bombs had also come down in our area. We wanted to see our house. As we were walking on the Cellerstrasse, almost a half kilometre away from the bunker and just at the 'Apostel Kirche' (Apostle church) on our right, we saw this low flying plane over the Lützerodestrasse coming towards us. When we first saw it, it was perhaps a half-kilometre away. It was machine-gunning the street. My mother yelled "into that house", she meant the house in front of us. I dropped my little suitcase and pillow and ran into the house. Just before we got into the house, the plane dropped a bomb right in the middle of the street, about 250 metres away from us. We ran down the stairs into the cellar. There was someone else in the cellar as well. When it was quiet for a while we concluded that this plane was just a straggler. We waited not more than five minutes before we left the cellar. I picked up my pillow and suitcase from the street and we went on towards our house. It was still standing. Often there would be a few windows broken, but they were replaced fairly quickly, in a day or two.

I don't recall being worried about getting killed or about losing the house, and I don't recall my mother expressing that she was worried about those things either. During the war years these two things were totally out of the hands of individuals like us. Our lives had become so much of a routine, and we had no control over it. There were so many people around us getting killed and losing their belongings on a weekly basis over the war years, without anyone having any control over the events. Every once in a while, somebody in our bunker cabin did not come back; I guess their houses were destroyed and they had to move into the country side.

In 1945, even after the bombardments of Hannover on January 5th and 10th, February 11th and March 3th, 14th, 15th and 17th, the worst I was to experience was still to come. On March 25th and 28th the British and American air forces, with 600 bombers each, conducted raids on my part of the city. Like the last air raid before this one, and just like hundreds of air raid alarms before, this one did not seem to be any different. We had a pre-alarm, and the radio announcement was that a large number of planes were flying in the direction of Hannover, with possible targets beyond it. We went into the bunker and waited. After perhaps an hour or less we felt the first bombs vibrating the bunker.

There must have been clear indications given over the radio after we had left the house that Hannover would be the target, because the bunker was just packed like sardines. I was sitting on the bench with people in our cabin standing so close that no one sitting would have been able to stand up. My knees were touching the legs of the people standing in front of me. All of a sudden all hell seemed to break loose. The bombs came closer and closer, and the lights went out. The emergency power never came on. The lights may have been out for five or ten minutes when the first bomb hit the bunker. I instantly felt like I had been thrown up a foot or two from my seat and then dropped back onto it. When it happened, I looked up in the pitch darkness of the cabin to see if the ceiling had split, but it hadn't. The whole bunker shook many times like never before. During that same time, two more direct hits to the bunker happened as well. The whole hell lasted for less than an hour. But the lights were off for hours and everyone was told to stay put for a long time. It was daytime by the time we were allowed to leave the bunker.

We exited by our regular outside first-floor side entrance. As we were going down the concrete stairs, with the railing gone, we saw these huge bomb craters, perhaps a dozen, all around the bunker. These craters were large enough to plunk bungalows into them. These must have been some of the largest Allied bombs, blockbusters, to be used in the Second World War. When we came around the corner of the bunker, we saw that the steel doors to the vestibule at the ground floor level were lying mangled outside, and the two inside steel doors were torn off and mangled as well. There was quite a bit of blood on the ground. We did not stop to look; what we saw was all in passing by. We had to walk over mounts of dirt thrown up by the bombs that made the craters. We also saw, along the side of the bunker that had no entrance, a long row of blankets that were covering something up. The row consisted of about thirty to forty blankets. We just rushed back to our house; again, except for all the windows being broken, it was fine.

The following night, when we had to go back to the bunker in the dark, we had to climb around the craters, and be careful not to fall into them. When we were in the bunker, we found out that all the blankets we had seen along the bunker the day before had been covering dead bodies. What happened during the raid was that some of the bombs were 'Luftminen' – blockbuster – bombs. These were special bombs, we were told, in that they created an implosion instead of an explosion. When they hit, they seemed to suck the air towards them and in that way had sucked the doors out of the bunker. Because the people suspected a raid on our district of Hannover, the bunker had been packed with more people than at any time before. They said that there had been 13,000 people in the bunker instead of the 10,000 that it had been designed for.

Because the inside was so packed, some people just stayed in the vestibules. They were standing like sardines between the outer and inner steel doors. When the air mines hit, the doors of the two ground level vestibules, and all the people in them, were sucked out, all mangled up. The blankets we saw the day before covered up the bodies of those people. It was amazing how fast these doors were replaced. Because the alarm siren went off again the next night, they found on the following day that some elderly people had fallen into the bomb craters and drowned. It was spring and the craters had filled up with ground water almost immediately. A couple of days later the craters were filled in with earth and levelled.

The Bombing Raid destruction of the Hannover city centre by100 squadron Lancaster. The aerial photograph was taken by Margaret Bourke-White (USAAF).

At the beginning of April, 1945, my sister's Pflichtjahr, the one year compulsory domestic service, was up and she was sent back home to Hannover. She was now fifteen and was told to report to the Employment Department office as soon as she got back to Hannover. So my mother and sister went together to that office, hoping that they would just forget about sending her somewhere. The Allied troops were already in Germany and the war would be over soon anyway. However, the office had no position for her to go to and consequently they wanted her to join the army as an anti-aircraft-gun helper. They were desperate to recruit new personnel to replace the ones killed. However, we were expecting the foreign troops to march into Hannover in a week or so anyway. When my sister and mother came home they were scared. My sister was only fifteen years old and she was to help firing flack cannons against the Allied planes that were all over us every day.

It just so happened that on that day a girl, I believe she was sixteen years old, had come from Schwüblingsen with her girlfriend, to return a ladies bicycle that my mother had lend to her brother some time ago. When the brother was drafted into the army and spent a couple of days in Hannover my mother allowed him to take the bike so he could go back to his parents in Schwüblingsen. When the girls heard what my sister was supposed to do they said that they would take her back to Schwüblingsen with them and that she would be safe there. The girl who wanted to bring the bike back was the daughter of a small farmer in Schwüblingsen and her mother was actually another godmother to my sister. So the three girls then shared two bikes between them on their way to Schwüblingsen. They shared riding the bike alternately and covered the 30 km distance in one day. According to my sister, they saw air attacks all around them. One portion of their travel was on the Autobahn, which left them very exposed to possible strafing by low flying Allied fighter planes. However, they arrived safe and well.

By the end of the war, Hannover, a city with a population of almost half a million which had had about 80 percent of its houses destroyed, suffered only 6,782 dead, equalling 1.4 percent of its population. This number of casualties was very small when compared to the seventeen worst-hit German cities that had more casualties, namely 522,444, or an average of 30,732 per city. Some of these cities were even much smaller than Hannover; however, their casualty rates were up in the twenty percent range. Some cities received only half or less the number of bombs dropped on them that Hannover had, however, their casualties were much greater. It appears that not all German cities were equally prepared in terms of having enough bomb shelters for their citizens. Many of these were perhaps not considered potential targets for Allied air attacks, because they didn't have any important industries, and, in some cases, no industries at all. But for the Allied Powers, hitting industries was secondary; the main aim was to demoralize the German population.

It was the 10th of April 1945 when, while we were in the bunker, there were rumours going around that American troops had entered the city. People were still afraid to go home because there always seemed to be planes in the area and the German communication system had ceased to function. Sometime in the morning that day we left the bunker; most people thought it was best to be at home when the foreign troops arrived. No one knew what to expect, there were so many rumours going around and some of them were quite horrific, women and young girls getting raped and places getting looted. By this time the Russians had already been on German soil for more than six months and there were many eyewitnesses who managed to get to Hannover, telling unbelievable stories.

The people thought it was a blessing to be in an area that was going to be conquered by the Americans. The rumour was that the troops would be coming into the city from the west; our district, the "List," was northeast of the city centre. So when we got outside the Welfenbunker, we looked down Cellerstrasse in the opposite direction from the one we would walk to get home. This was the direction from which we thought the troops would come into our area.

In the distance, almost a kilometre away, there was a long railway overpass. After a few minutes we could see through the street underpass that on Herschelstrasse tanks were crossing the Cellerstrasse from right to left. We assumed that they were American tanks. They were going towards the centre of Hannover, which is also where the huge railway station is.

We then turned around and went home. At home, everything was intact. There would be fighter planes flying overhead once in a while, but we did not hear any shooting. Around noon, my mother somehow found out that there was a store that was selling frozen fruit. By this time, the last few weeks of the war, food was becoming quite scarce. I then told my mother that I should go and see if I could get some of that fruit. She agreed and I took off down the "Alte Cellerheerstrasse" towards the central railway station.

The store I had to go to was a little over a kilometre away from our house and only a block away from the huge Hauptbahnhof (central railway station) of Hannover. When I got closer to the store, I saw a line-up of about twenty-five people, mainly women and children my age. I guess everybody was convinced that the American troops would not harm children. I got to the end of the line. The store had the door closed and only one person at a time would be let in to get something. As we were standing there, we started to hear some rumbling noises coming from the Hauptbahnhof. Shortly after, looking in the direction of the railway station, we saw a tank turning around the corner onto the Alte Cellerheerstrasse into the direction where we were. The star on it told us that it was an American tank. At that point it was about 150 metres from us. There were foot soldiers with their guns at the ready walking behind it. Then a second tank came into view. Right across the street from the store, where I was trying to get some frozen fruit, was a large five-storey prison building. The outside wall of the building was right along the street, and each floor had about ten cell windows facing the street. By now the inmates also realized what was happening, and they started yelling and whistling.

As the tanks came closer, some kids came out of the houses and greeted the soldiers. The Americans were throwing chocolates to the kids on the street. I stayed in my line-up. The inmates then started to let strings down out of their windows and the soldiers tied all kinds of things to them – cigarettes, chocolates and cans. The prison was at a street intersection. The corner of the prison building, facing the intersection, was blunt to accommodate the main prison entrance. Anyone looking out of that entrance would not have been able to see what went on along the section of the street where I was. All of a sudden two guards in uniform came running out of that prison entrance and ran across our street. It was only when they started running across that they realized that the American soldiers were only 50 metres away. Nevertheless, they ran into one of the houses next to the store, with American soldiers in hot pursuit. A minute or so later the guards came out with their hands up and the soldiers behind them. The inmates, who watched the whole thing from across the street, were cheering. Finally I got my frozen fruit package and walked home. The soldiers stayed put, I guess they had to look after the prison before going on.

Later on, a jeep would drive through the streets with loudspeakers blaring that people should stay home and not go into the streets until they would be told that they were allowed to. After that, a jeep loudspeaker warned us not to leave our homes at night. During the first two nights, there was some shooting in the neighbourhood and

fighter planes flying very low over the houses would also be shooting the odd times. The only people freely roaming the streets were
foreigners who had been brought to Germany by the Nazis to work
in factories or on farms. These roaming people did some looting
and smashing up of places, as well as raping women and young girls.
It scared the hell out of the German population, which consisted
mainly of women and children at this point. But this looting was
stopped by the American forces after a few days. I think it was on
the third day that we were allowed to go to the stores for a few hours
for food, whatever little food there was. However, we did get a lot
of rest, because of no more alarms to worry about. It was about a
month later when the war in Europe officially came to an end; on
May 7/8, 1945 the armistice was signed for all of Germany.

AFTERWORD

ABOUT THE BOMBINGS.

During the war there were 428 air raid alarms in my hometown, Hannover. One of the heaviest raids was a night raid from October 8th to 9th, 1943, when 3,000 high-explosive bombs, 28,000 phosphorous bombs and 230,000 incendiary bombs were dropped on Hannover. It was called "Black Day". It only killed 1,245 people; however it destroyed nearly 250,000 apartments, nearly 50 percent of the city's housing. Days later, another 23,051 tons of bombs fell on Hannover. This was an example of the carpet bombing of suburban and residential civilian targets laid out in the February 14, 1942 Area Bombing Directive. The Area Bombing Directive was a directive from the wartime British Government's Air Ministry to the Royal Air Force which ordered RAF bombers to attack the German industrial workforce and the morale of the German populace through bombing German cities and their civilian inhabitants.

By the end of the war, 6,782 people had been killed in Hannover. In comparison to other German cities it was a very small number. However, of the 147,222 buildings recorded before the war, only 7,498 were undamaged. In other words, 95 percent of the dwellings were destroyed or damaged. The population of Hannover in 1939 was 471,000 people; it fell to 217,000 by May of 1945. Still, one can only imagine how crammed together the remaining people had to live by the end of the war.

The total numbers of bombs dropped on Hannover during the war were;

Aerial Mines – Blockbusters	1,000
High Explosive Bombs	34,000
Phosphorous Bombs	50,000
Incendiary Bombs	900,000

The Hannover bombing statistics come from:

1. EUROPA im BOMBEN-FRIEG 1939-1945
   By Maximilian Czesany – Leopold Stocker Verlag

2. http://www.revisonist.net/bombed-cities-08.html

3. University of Exeter – Centre for the Study of War, State and Society –
   Bombing, States and Peoples in Western Europe 1940-1945
   The Bombing of Germany 1940 - 1945
   Allied air-strikes and civil mood in Germany

The Models below are displayed in the City Hall of Hannover.

This is what the downtown city Centre looked like in 1939.

This is what the downtown city Centre looked like in 1945.

CPSIA information can be obtained
at www.ICGtesting.com
Printed in the USA
LVHW090838100920
665445LV00012B/11/J